A
Martial Artist's Guide
To
Failing Your Way
To
Success

THE DAN-DO METHOD

Daniel Lee Bourelle

simply francis publishing company
North Carolina

This book is a memoir. However, some references to historical events, real people, or real places have been changed to protect for privacy as required by law.
Library of Congress Control Number:
ISBN: 978-1-63062-026-4 (paperback)
ISBN: 978-1-63062-027-1 (ebook)
Printed in the United States of America
Cover and Interior Design: Christy King Meares

For information about this title or to order books and/or electronic media, contact the publisher:

simply francis publishing company
P.O. Box 329, Wrightsville Beach, NC 28480
www.simplyfrancispublishing.com
simplyfrancispublishing@gmail.com

Dedication

This book is dedicated to the two most important people who have influenced my life, and also the two people that will never be able to read this book.

To my mother, Shirley Ann Bourelle, you gave me my passion for helping others and to not take things too seriously in life. I'm not sure how much of my memory of you is real, or if it's from the photos I keep and the stories others have told. However, I still remember your essence of love and laughter. I hope I represented it well in this book.

To my father, Raymond Eugene Bourelle, you led by example to instill in me an unparalleled work ethic, coupled with an iron will and strength to fight through the toughest parts of life where others would crumble. This too, I hope I represented well in this book.

TABLE OF CONTENTS

PREFACE

I've been wanting to write a book on martial arts for quite some time. Like most people attempting to accomplish something out of the ordinary from what they do, there was always something more urgent to deal with and the effort of writing placed low on the "To-Do" list.

In 2004, after moving to Wilmington, North Carolina from Norfolk, Nebraska and starting up my own martial arts school, I created my first website. It was awful. Like an eight-year-old attempting to draw the Mona Lisa with a crayon level of awful. However, I filled it with some content that would lead me to writing this book years later. I labelled that content as, "Myths and Misconceptions of Martial Arts" and wrote up some basic, and bland articles on the matter.

In late 2011, one of my earliest promoted black belts, David, offered up his web design services to revamp my website. He, unlike myself, actually had Michelangelo level of talent when it comes to web design and he made, far and away, the best martial arts website I've ever seen. After the launch, he told me I needed to constantly update the site to keep it high up on the search engines and mentioned a blog would be the easiest way to make that happen. I finally had my reason to start writing that book!

I began by writing two blog articles each month - one martial arts related and one fitness related. I decided early on that the martial arts related ones would eventually become chapters of my book. Nine short years later, my book is finally finished - yes, nine years. Slow and steady wins the race, right?

Essentially, I just decided to take what I wrote and compile it into a book, even if I have more to write. I'm somewhat addicted to the writing process, admittedly, as it's been not only therapeutic in some regards but has completely cured the insomnia I've had my entire life. I spent years trying new drugs from the doctors trying to fix my insomnia, as well as, going down checklists of what to do before bed.

I started running regularly when I first moved to Wilmington and that helped in the beginning, but I couldn't outrun the insomnia for long as it eventually seeped back in. After the first blog I wrote and posted, I fell asleep instantly. It was as if it organized and filed away the thoughts that swirled around my head every night I lay my head down. While I'll continue to write to keep the insomnia demons at bay, I've decided to place a bookmark on my writing to finally compile, edit, and publish this book.

I've separated this book into something most martial artists will relate to in regards to their training. The body, the mind, and the spirit. These are three things we must focus on to truly develop into an experienced martial artist and even a well-rounded person. Not every martial artist attains development in these in the same order.

I find most people will focus on adjusting the physical body as it's the easiest to understand how to fix. The mind is considerably harder. We all tend to know that our mindset can hold us back, but knowing how to do so is a different story. The spirit, for most, is the hardest to understand, let alone adjust. I'm reminded of the "void" or "no-thing-ness" that is discussed in *The Book of Five Rings*, authored by Miyamoto Musashi. It's not necessarily anything spiritual nor religious. In my book I relate it more towards emotion or an invisible driving force.

Try not to think too hard about it as all the parts are more about observing and recognizing potential attributes and to adjust it if you feel it isn't working for you. If nothing else, I hope you enjoy some of the stories and maybe laugh a little at my own failures.

One thing I've learned in my years of training and teaching martial arts is that I change my mind on things constantly. I'm willing to bet that in twenty years' time, I could re-write or add to much of the topics in this book. So take nothing I've written as gospel, only as my thoughts at this time to promote thought, even if they sound a little preachy. Even between the time I've written some of these as blogs and the time I've compiled them into this book, I've adjusted and re-written portions of the text. Nothing is set in stone and everything is constantly evolving. I just hope I'm not embarrassed by any of it years later! Inevitably, I decided to write these excerpts, and what is now a book, hoping to reach more than just my students, even though they were my audience at the time.

> *"You can always count on the Americans to do the right thing, after they have exhausted all the other possibilities."*
> *– Winston Churchill (supposedly, but not a proven quote)*

In the above quote, you could easily change "the Americans" to "Daniel." As I say in these pages, I've made an unnecessary number of mistakes and failures in life and in martial arts. My life experiences inspired many chapters and are the reason I've settled on the title of this book. My father once told me when I was younger that if there were one hundred people in a back yard and one pile of dog poop, I would be the one to step in the poop! That was fine, though, as I would then be more cautious of where I stepped in the future. While everyone else mistakenly walked off a cliff by not paying attention, I would see it coming and go around safely.

A couple friends of mine called these strange, poop-stepping moments as, "Dan moments". This has morphed into the Dan-Do method for this book and was the catalyst for its formation. "Dan-Do" is a bit of a play on words. While Dan in Korean essentially means rank, in regard to the book, it is just my name. "Do" in Korean is associated with, "The Way." Hence it is known as, "The Way of Dan".

My way is apparently constantly failing in an effort to succeed. I've lived my life on a trial and error process. Why measure twice and cut once when I can measure once and cut twice because cutting is the fun part, that's what I say! Emphasis on the error portion of "trial and error" as you'll discover throughout these pages. I hope the reader will find something useful, whether you're into martial arts or not, even if it's just to solidify your own training or experiences. At the very least, I hope you just enjoy reading it!

PROLOGUE

Failure is not an option – It's mandatory

In the martial arts, failure is inevitable. Not because it is especially difficult; but rather because the martial arts are founded upon discovering and attempting to reach your potential by realizing your weaknesses. We hope to strengthen these weaknesses - whether it be physically, mentally, or spiritually. Martial arts *will* find your weaknesses and force you to fail.

When a student is ready to test for their first degree black belt at my dojang, the Korean name of a training facility, I put them through the wringer. Knowing, understanding and performing their set rank material is just a portion of that test. Each student has a different reason for practicing the martial arts and carries with him different talents and struggles. Because of this, not every black belt testing is the same. For those who are quiet and lacking in confidence, I have them write a speech on their martial arts journey. I then have them give that speech in front of everyone in attendance.

For others, self-defense is their biggest reason for training. I put them through a gauntlet of difficult self-defense scenarios. Another student may have a phobia of spiders or heights. These students will be placed on a ladder while I throw live tarantulas at them. Okay, so this one hasn't actually happened yet, but you better believe I've written it down in my upcoming book *How to Train Students through Massive Torture.*

Aside from customizing the testing to the student's goals in training, I set up a way to make them fail at testing. Usually, this is accomplished through sparring - massive amounts of sparring. It could go on for thirty minutes or even an hour. I do whatever it takes to make them reach the point where their brain has put up the vacancy sign, walked out the door, and shown no signs of ever returning. I'm waiting for this moment of failure so that their real testing can begin.

Anyone can perform well when comfortable or in their prime moment of being. When it comes to self-defense, "at your peak" is the least likely time to be attacked. It happens when we have been walking around the streets all day in the hot sun on vacation, dehydrated, hungry, head aching, kids screaming in your ear, wishing for blissful death to take you away. That is when we are at our most vulnerable. An attacker strikes when they know we are the least likely to fight back. I look to break students down to that absolute vulnerability when we spar at their rank testing. After I see that, we proceed to test their skills and demonstrate what is truly engrained in them from all the years of training.

Do these students need to win every match? No. Do they need to avoid every hard hit coming in? No. Do they have to perform at their best? No. Do they just have to not give up? Yes. It is amazing what the body can do when the brain has left the building but the body has been trained properly. I have seen pulled muscles, broken fingers and toes, bloody noses, and swollen eyes during testing, but the one thing they cannot do is quit. No matter the odds, the student has to keep going. This is when I discover who deserves that black belt or not.

Enmanual Tejada after breaking his nose early on during a round robin tournament in which he finished all of his matches even with a broken nose.
Photographer: Jen Van Kirk

Almost all of my students collapse in exhaustion the second I call out that final, "Break!" As long as they did not stop before then, in all likelihood they will have earned their black belt.

Surprisingly, most students do quite well physically after that failure point. The body knows what to do and can continue to do it, even if the brain already checked out. This failure point also shows students (and me) where their mistakes lay and where they can improve in future classes. It's easy to cover up weaknesses when the brain functions properly, but not so much when it's toast.

This is why it's so important to fail. Students learn a lot about themselves when they get pushed to fail. I can predict where those mistakes will happen and could easily tell the student. However, it's not until the student experiences this failure that they fully understand their shortcomings and can adjust to overcome these mistakes. Becoming a black belt is not about being the best, a student must understand that they are not the best and still progress in a clear direction toward their goals.

Even though we do everything we can to avoid failure, we will never fully appreciate our achievements and successes without it. We would never realize our shortcomings and weaknesses, and therefore, never improve our ability to reach greater achievements and successes. Through failure, we understand our limits. When we know our limits, we can reach our fullest potential.

We've all heard the saying, "When you fall off the horse, dust yourself off and climb back on." What we tend to forget is that in order to get back on the horse after falling, is that we first have to get on the horse to begin with. This is where most fail. Unfortunately, this is one failure that doesn't lead to success. So find your horse, climb on, and know that you will fall eventually, but also know you'll be better off for it.

PART 1:

Observations of the Body

CHAPTER 1

Don't dip your toes in the water and claim you're a swimmer

Patience, it's a must. We all need it, yet seemingly few of us have it. While this is common knowledge, I thought I would take a different route when it comes to talking about patience. I read an excellent book a few years ago called, *"The Art of Harmony"* by author and martial artist Sang H. Kim. I came across a section about perseverance. In particular, the perseverance of a spider, which triggered a thought about patience. Some people rely too much on patience when it is not needed. Allow me to explain.

One of the most patient creatures on Earth is the common garden spider. Why? Because it has to be. It delicately and tediously spins its web to perfection, then patiently waits for its food. It has no choice. Its survival depends on being patient. The garden spider created a masterpiece which, with patience, led to food and survival.

What is the least patient creature on the planet? The human being. We don't need to be as patient as the common garden spider. We have all the tools necessary to get what we need and fairly quickly, especially this day and age.

Does that mean we do not need patience? Of course not.

Not everything can be acquired quickly. Many things in life still require patience. What I want to focus on, though, is relying on patience to create something from nothing. Over the years, occasionally students do nothing more than show up to class and patiently wait to get better - as if the skill and talent will suddenly appear out of thin air one day. They missed a key ingredient in the success formula.

They forgot to build their masterpiece.

While showing up to class is an important step in the learning process, by no means is it the only step in the process. We must constantly work hard to achieve our goals. Simply showing up is not enough to accomplish what we want to accomplish.

We must also understand that the goal is not to acquire skill; but rather it is to build skill to acquire success. Skill is our web, our masterpiece, but not our food. Any time we go to class, to work, or wherever we go to create our success, we need to remember to spin our web first.

My father, Raymond Eugene Bourelle or Gene to his friends and "Yes, Sir, Father, Sir!" as my brothers and I were forced to call him (I'm joking, of course, only one Sir was needed) grew up helping his parents run the family farm on the eastern side of Nebraska. After high school, my father decided he wanted to go to college and become a mechanic. He went to college in Kansas City, Kansas, which was about a five hour drive from the farm at the time. He went to school full time, worked when not in class during the week in order to pay for college, and drove that five hours back to his family's farm every Friday evening to help on the farm all weekend. He then drove the five hours back late Sunday evening to be back in class Monday morning.

He did that every week until he got his degree in Auto Mechanics, which landed him his first career related job with Chrysler®. This led to teaching Automotives at the college in the town I grew up in, and then to being the Dean of Heavy Construction before retiring at the age of 65. He then became a part time claims adjuster, climbing ladders to walk around on roofs and constantly remodeling his house with his own hands on the weekends, in between well-deserved golfing and fishing trips.

Clearly, lacking effort is not something I would ever use to describe my father.

He placed 100% effort into everything he did in life and never waited for things to fall into his lap. He had a clear vision of what he wanted to obtain and placed all of his efforts into securing that goal. It took me some time while growing up to understand what it was that made my father so successful.

In order from left to right: Melvin Bourelle (Dan's uncle), Raymond Bourelle (Dan's grandfather), Gene Bourelle (Dan's father)

I participated in all the major sports as a child. Basketball, bowling, football, wrestling, golf, and last but not least, my first love, baseball. I grew up in a very athletic family, so it was normal to be playing some sort of sport or athletic activity all year round. I loved playing, but desperately wanted to be the best and to win first place in everything. Regrettably, I have the world's largest collection of second place trophies. I competed in martial arts for years, and this also, left me with an unnerving number of second and third place trophies.

Around 2002, shortly after college, I stopped virtually everything and focused solely on martial arts. I sparred fellow students for an extra hour or two after class. I practiced constantly at home. I even used my stretching machine every day to get close to being able to do the splits, which granted me more options and combinations to add to my offensive arsenal. I also began bringing a camcorder with me, politely asking fellow attending students to record video of my competitions and reviewing them for ways to improve. I also spent more time in the gym, stopped drinking soda, and cleaned up my nutrition and pre-tournament breakfast.

Who knew Pop- Tarts® and soda were not the breakfast of champions?

That year, I began taking home first place trophies on a regular basis. I began to realize that natural talent, *sans* training effort, wasn't going to cut it. I learned that there is always someone out there that has the same talent, but with more drive and effort that will always beat me. My effort had to change.

I recall years ago, going to the grocery store and asking the stock clerk where an item is located. He was able to tell me exactly where it was, specials going on, and the difference between two different brands or styles of an item. Try that today and the stock clerk, most likely, won't even take the time to look at you to tell you that they don't know, or maybe it's "over yonder" or that it's not their job. I hate to sound like the old guy complaining that things were better in my day, but it seems like we've lost the pride and effort in our work and are bombarded with so many other things pulling our attention away.

It's tough to blame anyone though as there has been a pretty major shift in our lives over the years. There seems to be no such thing as a stable job or career anymore, which leads us to studying backup skills and not placing all of our focus on any one thing. The recession in 2008 made that very clear. Nearly everyone I know has either multiple jobs or one major job with a side hustle or two, or five. It's all but needed these days with all the uncertainty. Sadly, because of this, it seems that so few place all of their pride and effort into their professions.

On the flip side, there are a lot of positive things that may have led to this as well. With the internet and smart phones, we have access to any and all information within minutes. So why hire a professional to install your sink when YouTube™ can teach you how to fumble your way through it for slightly less cost? Many of us are becoming jacks of all trades, yet masters of nothing. While it's great to have multiple skill sets to save some money, there is an issue with this as it leads us to spreading out our focus to numerous jobs rather than honing in on our one great skill set. This can lead to mistakes in our professions.

For example, a mother came to me years ago wanting to get her daughter some personal training to lose weight. We sat down and discussed her daughter's background, when she began gaining weight and what her goals were, among other things. "She had been a very happy child up until about a year ago," the mother claimed. "She was athletic and in good shape when she competed in sports. Then suddenly she began gaining weight and has since become depressed about her weight gain."

I dove in a little further, attempting to get to the moment things changed. The mother believed her daughter began gaining weight when she quit her favorite sport and yet she was eating very clean, healthy food. I need to point out, the daughter at this point, had over fifty percent body fat. The average fourteen-year-old girl has about fifteen percent. That means she gained about thirty five percent body fat in about a year. This doesn't happen when you simply stop competing in sports. Even adding in a considerable amount of food won't add that much weight in that little time, especially at that age.

There had to be more to this story, so I continued to dig. Why would the daughter quit her favorite sport suddenly? Finally, I began to get some answers. The mother, in passing, mentioned divorcing the daughter's father, about a year ago. This is what inevitably led to quitting sports.

I then turned my attention to the daughter, asking what her day was like when she stayed with her father. Essentially, the father fed her candy and junk food all day, as he didn't know how to cook and all he had was junk food. Still, the math just wasn't adding up, but we were getting closer to the real answer. A lack of exercise and the addition of junk food on the weekends still doesn't equate to over 100 pounds of weight being gained in a year. I then asked a question that provided an answer that has dumbfounded me and upset, nay, angered me, to this very day. I asked about any medications.

There were a couple, but one in particular. They had gone to the doctor about the daughter's depression. The doctor provided an anti-depressant. This particular anti-depressant had a specific side effect...weight gain. That's right, when the doctor heard that the daughter was depressed about being overweight, he prescribed an anti-depressant that would cause her to gain more weight, but be happy about it. I'll wait while you finish slapping your hands to your heads and losing faith in our doctors. This astonishing lack of effort in such an important profession leads people to not trusting that profession. That mistrust spreads to assuming mistrust in other professions. Flat Earthers, climate deniers, anti-vaxxers, anti-science, and so on, are a result of this lack of trust in professionals. I may disagree with the above mentioned, but when so many seem to slack off in their professions, it's understandable why people no longer trust authority figures. And then there's the martial arts instructor...

This isn't to say that everyone should stick to one skill and never expand out. These days we need multiple skill sets just to get by. I know very few martial arts instructors that make their living solely as a martial arts instructor. In my case, I am also a personal trainer, part time. What I'm getting at is that we need to be honest with ourselves, our knowledge and skills, as well as to have pride in what we do. You'd think a profession where there is an actual rank labelled as, "Master," would be better known for actually being masters of their profession. Yet, not all are.

Understandably so, however, as it's insanely difficult to make money running a martial arts studio. I've seen far too many martial arts instructors teach that which they don't fully understand due to this lack of honesty with themselves and lack of training effort. This isn't just bad, it's flat out dangerous. Martial arts is teaching self-defense for times when your life is on the line. Acting like a master when you are closer to a novice is immoral and irresponsible.

Training students to defend themselves in a way that may be wrong due to your lack of knowledge can lead to serious injury or death. This is how watered-down versions of martial arts get produced. These watered-down versions of martial arts are like a cancer on the martial arts world. One bad instructor promotes a less than stellar student in a year or two to their black belt and sends them off to teach, further watering down and misinterpreting the art. I can't begin to tell you how frustrating this is as an instructor who places a lot of effort into teaching and continuing education. The average person seeking out training doesn't know the difference between a teacher who received his black belt by attending a seminar over the weekend and a true martial arts master who has dedicated his life to understanding the art of self-defense.

I've trained every day since 1994 in the same arts and I'm only now, in 2020, starting to feel like I may be deserving of the title "Master." I continue to train and learn from anyone, anywhere I can. With all of that said, I don't feel every martial arts instructor should only train in martial arts and not hold another job. That would kill most schools as it's insanely difficult to build a school that pays the bills as martial arts is HEAVILY under-valued by the public.

The issue, when it comes to running a successful full-time martial arts studio, is that you must spend a considerable amount of time studying business rather than your art just to keep the doors open. Hence, the reason there are so few high-quality martial arts schools that are full time. There are some, however, and my hats off to them. I hope to be them someday! Luckily, most martial arts instructors I know and have met, truly love training and teaching. They take considerable pride in what they do. They are also honest with themselves and what they are teaching. Why it's not ALL of them though, I don't know.

I have had students that train nearly every day and I've had students that train once a week. I place zero judgment on any of them as I respect anyone that puts any amount of effort into learning martial arts. So few do. The amount of times you show up to class is not the biggest indicator of who will make it to black belt or make noticeable improvements. Though it definitely helps if a student can make it to class multiple times a week. It all comes down to effort.

We have a saying in our Taekwondo class when it comes to the forms/patterns. Every technique in the form is the THE most important technique in the form. The point is that one technique is not more important than the other. So when I ask to see a student's form, I expect 100% power and effort into each movement. If you're not breathing heavy and need a brief rest after performing your form, you didn't place enough effort into the techniques. I know everything I need to know about the student's mindset and effort just by seeing that form.

I'm accepting of mistakes in forms if I see the student is putting all of their effort into it. That shows me that all that stands in the way from the student progressing is effort and time on my part, which is my pleasure to give. However, if the student shows me bare minimum effort and seems more interested in the butterfly outside, I know they have no interest in improving with hard work and I simply say, "Try harder next time."

Lack of effort is among my biggest pet peeves. Not every student will have natural physical ability. Not every student can learn quickly. However, every student can put effort into what they do. So many things these days are easily accessible due to the internet. We can quickly learn or access most anything instantly. I fear it leads people to assume that they will obtain martial arts adeptness just by showing up or casually going through their material. This couldn't be further from the truth. There is no fast track to black belt or mastering an art or a technique. Though I yearn for the day we can just download to our brain a new skill. For now though, the only path is through massive amounts of effort. Again, it's the one thing that everyone can do, give effort. If you do that, I'll keep helping and will love you as a student.

In regards to obtaining a black belt, understand that lollygagging through class won't cut it. Even those who place everything they have into their training can struggle obtaining that highly sought after rank. Also, understand that obtaining a black belt doesn't have to be the ultimate goal. I hope that most students I teach recognize and obtain so much more from their training than just their rank. And I believe most of my students do. However, a slacker's approach will never garner anything more than a new color belt around your waist from time to time before halting once getting into the intermediate ranks, if that far. Memorizing technique and regurgitating it may get you through the first few ranks, but after that, it must be applied and understood and performed on a higher level each time you move up in rank.

The ultimate point of this chapter is to be honest with yourself on your level of effort and the pride you place in your work and training, student or instructors alike. As long as you recognize your output and knowledge level, then you'll be fine. If you want to truly be a martial artist, put all of your effort into it. Take time to practice at home, even if that means just reading through notes from classes or looking over videos you took of your last training session to critique. Maybe visualizing punching and choking out your neighbor for being too loud and driving excessively fast where kids are playing, and letting their untrained and large dog roam free, defecating on your yard and chasing after you while taking your dog on a walk...uh, anyway, stop reading and go practice right now! And try and avoid assaulting your neighbors.

CHAPTER 2

Golf, shelves, and martial arts

An elite golfer, a high ranking martial artist and a hand crafted book shelf walk into a bar...

Follow me on this, those three things do connect. I once had someone tell me a story about a few golfers on a driving range. As the story goes, a golfer on the range is repeatedly hitting bad shots. His feet were all wrong, his hips had improper movement, his arms flailed horribly out of control and he constantly pulled his head not seeing the ball. Two other golfers walk by noticing the bad technique and consistent inconsistency of the hits. The one golfer then turned to the other and said, "I wonder why he's practicing like that for? It's clearly not working."

I found this story to be especially funny considering I am a personal trainer and martial arts instructor. I see people seemingly practice horrible technique with no intent on improvement. Some know they have bad technique and just assume it will correct itself over time, others simply don't know its bad technique. Both continue practicing bad technique and wonder why they aren't seeing improvement. One must actively attempt to improve on technique to achieve success of their goals.

Remember those peers from high school that seemed to be naturally good at any sport, put no effort into anything, yet still succeeded? Where are they now? Did they succeed in life as they did in everything else they did when they were younger? Many have not. Why? Because there was no hard work put into their success. Therefore, there was no appreciation for the success they received. This leads to a lack of incentive to work hard.

Doing well at higher levels of a sport calls for hard work. At the elite levels, everyone is a natural freak. They no longer stand out like they once did. When it comes to adult life and careers natural talent doesn't do much if there is no hard work behind it. This obviously doesn't apply to everyone, but it does apply to most. The point being that without hard work, there is no appreciation for success, and with no appreciation for success, there is no repeat of success. There is no lasting success. There is no contentment or enjoyment that comes with success. There is no sense of worth. Worse yet, there is a sense of entitlement. When one inevitably fails at something, they are crushed by the failure. Those who consistently work hard understand that failure happens, and is an important part of the learning process that helps foster further success.

This leads me to the book shelf. Think of the book shelf (or any piece of furniture or object in your home) that you purchased from a store. If you suddenly had no books to place in it, would you keep it? What if you needed some cash? What if it breaks? Most of us would either toss out that book shelf or sell it as soon as it has no use. Now think of the book shelf (or again, any furniture or object) in your home that you yourself built with your own two hands. What would the answers to the above questions be?

For most of us, if you had no books for it, you would place objects on the shelf to make use of it. If you needed to sell some things for cash, it would be the last item on the list. If it broke, you'd fix it, or like most, put it aside with intent to fix it later! No matter what happens though; you would fight to keep it, would you not? What's the difference between the two? Chances are the factory built shelf is better in most ways, yet you still keep the one you made. It's because of hard work. You yourself put effort and hard work into that shelf. You didn't just create a shelf; you created a work of art. You created success. You created a sense of accomplishment.

You created an attachment to something that you are proud of. That shelf doesn't just hold up books, it holds up your pride and a sense of worth and is a display of a hard fought victory!

Many of us go through life doing just enough to get by. We study just enough to get a passing grade. We work just hard enough to not get fired. We do just enough to retain our spouses or significant others. Doing just enough does not equal success, it equals not failing. Hard work is what equals success, pride, self-worth, and strong relationships. I find the same obstacle over and over again when it comes to training others to work hard with maximum effort, and that's the fact that most associate hard work with a negative view such as pain, frustration and stress to name a few. While those things can be attached to hard work, it doesn't always have to be. Ask anyone who has been in a long, loving and happy marriage or relationship, most will tell you the same thing, they work hard at it and they enjoy working hard at it. Even if hard work does involve pain, frustration and stress, that just makes the accomplishment that much more rewarding. I'm reminded of a quote by Mohammad Ali on this subject. He was quoted as saying, "I hated every minute of training, but I said, don't quit. Suffer now and live the rest of your life as a champion."

I want to pass along something my father, as well as the rest of my family, instilled in me. Work ethic. I remember building a dog house with my father when I was younger. When he mentioned building the dog house, my assumption was to nail six pieces of plywood together and cut a hole in it. Boy was I wrong. We spent days, if not weeks on that dog house: two by fours across the bottom with a cut edge for easy sliding, a solid floor and foundation complete with floor joists and Fiberglass insulated studded walls. A twelve by twelve pitched roof with shingles. A doggy door with metal framing to keep it from cracking. A RIDICULOUS amount of nails to keep it all together. Lastly, it was topped off with a paint job to match our own home's color. It looked amazing!

The dog house Dan and his father built for his dog, Prince - A chocolate lab mix

Once finished, it was time to move it into the back yard. This dog house now weighed at least 500 pounds, so moving it wasn't that easy, but with a little more hard work, we got it out there. I was proud of that dog house, and I knew it wasn't going anywhere. Not just because I didn't want to get rid of it, but because that thing was built to withstand a nuclear bomb.

While nailing in the 300 millionth nail, I remember asking my father, "Why are we putting so much work into this dog house?"

He replied, "Whatever you do, do it the best you can and take pride in what you do."

Sounds simple, but so few people put this much effort into anything they do, let alone a simple dog house. So my advice to you, everything you do today, do it the best you can, and do it better than you did it yesterday. You just might build something more than what you expected.

...The elite golfer, the high ranking martial artist, and the hand crafted book shelf all ask the bartender for the same thing, "We would like a glass of the greatest drink ever made!" So the bartender handed all three an empty glass and said, "Then you'll have to create it yourself."

CHAPTER 3

The option

Dan (left), Brent Oravits (middle), and Todd Champion (right), after a sparring session. Photo by Alison Jean Gong

Daniel: Hey - you ever get into fights when you were a kid?

Miyagi: Huh - plenty.

Daniel: Yeah, but it wasn't like the problem I have, right?

Miyagi: Why? Fighting fighting. Same same.

Daniel: Yeah, but you knew karate.

Miyagi: Someone always know more.

Daniel: You mean there were times when you were scared to fight?

Miyagi: Always scare. Miyagi hate fighting.

Daniel: Yeah, but you like karate.

Miyagi: So?

Daniel: So, karate's fighting. You train to fight.

Miyagi: That what you think?

Daniel: [*pondering*] No.

Miyagi: Then why train?

Daniel: [*thinks*] So I won't have to fight.

Miyagi: [*laughs*] Miyagi have hope for you.

Who remembers this conversation? I'm guessing anyone over the age of twelve is nodding their head right now. If you're like me, you loved the Karate Kid movies from the eighties, but this conversation used to confuse me. I learn to fight, so I don't have to fight. I struggled for years trying to understand that thought process. Maybe it was my youth, maybe I just didn't hear it correctly, or maybe I was just naive. I just couldn't wrap my brain around why someone would learn a skill, then not want to use it.

Like many martial artists, I spent much of my early years training to be the best and trying to fill all the holes and weaknesses in my techniques to take on anyone and win. All that went through my mind was being the best fighter in the world. Not only did I feel like I could defend myself in any situation, I welcomed that mugger to jump out and test me. While I never really had one single moment of clarity, I slowly began to understand what the martial arts were about through teaching others. Ultimately, martial arts are about self-improvement. Not everyone trains for self-defense these days. However, when it comes to self-defense, an important aspect is creating the option not to fight.

If you learn to fight, yet choose not to, then there was no point in learning, correct? Wrong. Life is about having options, whether or not you choose them has no bearing. This is what "freedom" and "free will" are all about. The option to choose. When you take away your options, you take away your freedom to do as you see fit in your life. That's not living, that's surviving. When you only have a few dollars in your pocket and you need to eat, do you have a choice to buy a lobster? No, you buy the salad or a sandwich (or ramen noodles and a can of beer if you're a college student). Does that mean you would have bought a lobster if you had more money? No, you may have really wanted that sandwich. Wouldn't it be nice to have that option though? Yes!!!!

This is the option you are given when you learn martial arts. When given the opportunity to defend yourself or walk away, you now have a choice. Those who have no training, have no choice, even if their life depends on it. This country is built on having options and the freedom to choose, but it's up to us to create these options. If not, our only choice then becomes choosing not to have options. You are then left living a life you have to live, rather than the one you want to live.

This is the essence of what the wise old Mr. Miyagi was explaining in that unforgettable scene. Once again, martial arts transcends fighting. It's a reflection of life!

What happens when life puts an obstacle in your way? Did you create options for yourself to go the way you want to go so you can live the way you want to live? Or will you be forced to take a route and just survive?

One day years ago, my father, my brother, and I went fishing on a small lake just outside of our hometown. We jumped into my father's small fishing boat and eventually tied up at an old dead tree in the middle of the lake. My brother decided to grab a rod and climb out onto the dead tree sticking out of the water and fish from there, while my father and I stayed in the boat. We caught diddly squat. So we decided to try a new location and my brother started climbing back out of the tree to get back into the boat, then *Whoop! Splash!* Into the water he went! He was wearing sandals and slipped on the moss on the tree and fell in. None of us had life jackets on, mind you.

My dad was immediately stricken with fear, shock, and worry, and I....I....I had tears in my eyes I laughed so hard. My brother popped back out of the water and into the boat. I continued to laugh hysterically. Then my brother laughed. Our father was still a little in shock. Why the stark contrast between my father's reaction and mine? Did I see something he didn't? Did he see something I didn't? Was my dad a caring father and I a sociopathic jerk? Nope...well, sometimes, but not in this case.

The answer lies in an option my brother and I had that our father didn't. My brother and I knew how to swim, our father did not. I saw him fall in the water and not hit his head and knew he would just pop right back up and get in the boat. Our father, who couldn't swim, not only didn't know if my brother could swim back up and get out of the water, but also couldn't do anything to save him as he was unable to dive into the water if the situation called for it. So he sat in fear of not having the option to do anything. I knew, even if my brother didn't come back up right away, that I could jump in and get him and all would be fine. This is why having options is so important. I didn't need to use that option, but it gave me calmness, and hysterical laughter, while the lack of that option nearly gave my father a heart attack. We can tell ourselves how we don't need a certain skill set all we want, but using that skill is not the only reason to have it reside in you. Having options gives you peace of mind because you have choices.

Todd Champion (left) and Dan (right) sparring during class.
Photo by Alison Jean Gong

"The great general wins the war before he even fights the battle. But the first requirement is that you have to have an army. That's what training is, to become an army. You first have to be willing and able to fight. That comes first, then you choose not to, and it becomes the last thing you want to do. In order for it to be the last thing you want to do, it has to be the first thing you train for."
"...you only have a choice if you are able to do it. Otherwise it's just something you can't do and it has nothing to do with a choice."
– an interview with Paul Gale in Nei Jia Quan by Jess O'Brien

CHAPTER 4

A rocket propelled infant always ends in disaster!

Student, Fisher Read, attempting to get the attention of other students for a class photo. Photo by Jen Van Kirk

We learn to crawl before we walk. We learn to walk before we run. We learn to run before competing in track and field. We don't throw a newborn on the track expecting it to win the race, or even move for that matter. This is obvious stuff. Everything has order and structure to it to create progress. We have to remember this when it comes to learning something new or adjusting our lives in any way. Yet, everyone nowadays seems to want the end result immediately.

Want to walk into my classroom and forgo the balance, coordination, and foundational skills and go right into learning a jump spinning hook kick? Sure. Would you like to purchase the neck brace and pain killers now or after you fall and injure yourself? Want to lose fifty pounds of fat in a month? No problem, I have some pills for you and the number to a good doctor that will staple your stomach and give you liposuction. Then I'll see you back in three months when you've gained it all back since you never learned to change your habits that got you there in the first place.

One of my biggest frustrations is explaining to people that you can't simply fly through martial arts and attain your black belt in quick fashion. Most folks have unrealistic expectations in this matter. Yes, I can teach you how to do that jump spin hook kick. Yes, I can help you lose fifty pounds. The issue lays within your timeline.

One of the most common phone calls and email questions I get is, "Do you offer any self-defense only classes? Preferably a seminar or two to learn everything?" First of all, I love that someone is seeking out self-defense and I never get upset over that and always try and cater to their needs. I do have to be honest with them, however, and let them know that a seminar or short course by itself won't give you enough to be able to defend yourself unless you take that information and not only practice it daily, but expand on it considerably. This is what martial arts is all about. I'm not sure when our society decided martial arts and self-defense were two different things, but they aren't. Martial arts is the process of learning self-defense. Sadly, even though I beg seminar participants to continue training at home or at my studio or someone else's studio, only about two percent actually do.

So why do we have these expectations of *I want it and I want it now!?* Because we're in an age where we can have most everything right here, right now. With enough money, you can get just about anything you want, and quickly. We also have these so called "reality" TV shows that produce amazing results each and every week. Unfortunately, a TV week isn't exactly the same as a real life week.

Sorry, that weight loss show contestant didn't just lose twenty pounds in one week. They also don't have jobs to go to or kids to deal with during their time on the show. They live each day during the show doing nothing but working out and starving themselves among other unhealthy things just to produce a dramatic number for TV ratings. I know, it's a shocker, TV isn't real, who knew?

Online shopping, overnight delivery, cheap phone calls across the country, real time video chat, precooked and processed meals. It's no wonder we're lazy and want everything instantly; we've pretty well accomplished doing so in every way imaginable. Martial arts and fitness has yet to make that leap into instant attainment. At least not until we develop the Matrix and can just download information to enhance our performance. But last I checked, that's at least five years away, hah!

Consumers want that instant attainment, even if it isn't healthy or does no good. The end result seems to be more important than the journey, even if it's a false end result. I've been to far too many martial arts schools that all but sell black belts. Students flying through the ranks and being "awarded" their black belt in a years' time simply because it brings in money and keeps students happy. When a student enters my school and finds that it will take numerous years to earn a black belt, it's immediate disappointment for many.

Why does it take so long? Yes, I can teach you how to do that jump spin hook kick the first day. Yes, I can show you how to lose twenty pounds in a week. I can also strap a rocket to that newborn baby's back and have him cross the finish line first. I just won't. It's not safe, it accomplishes nothing, it's not smart, and it does no good whatsoever. Does losing that twenty pounds in a week improve your health? Nope, most likely hurts it if it's done that fast. Does learning that jump spin hook kick mean you can now defend yourself? Nope, you'll most likely fall on your keister and get laughed at, right before you get pummeled.

It's critical to build a base and a foundation when it comes to martial arts and fitness. In martial arts we spend endless hours teaching a student body control, self-awareness, and balance before we throw you into a sparring match. In fitness we start with core exercises to build a strong spine and strong joints to support us while doing bigger exercises. All of this leads to fewer injuries, quicker progress in the long run, and sustainable results. Yes, it's tougher and it takes longer, but it also means more to you when you accomplish your goals. This also means you're less likely to give up and more likely to sustain your goals.

Stop strapping a rocket to your back attempting to get your infantile skill to the finish line, you're just cheating yourself. Did you learn nothing from the turtle and the hare? Personally I thought the rabbit just lost due to his cockiness, but still, the moral of the story is slow and steady wins the race!

CHAPTER 5

I challenge you to a form-off!

*Men's and women's Warrior Cup III trophies awarded during the annual
tournament fundraiser hosted at Bourelle Martial Arts. Photo by Jen Van Kirk*

If you're not a martial artist, you may not get much from this
chapter. If you are into martial arts though, hopefully you'll come
away with a little more appreciation for form work and even help
boost your own forms training.

My first experience in forms training came from Taekwondo.
I didn't think much about it at the time. I just did the moves my
instructor told me to do, did it the best I could when tested, and
focused on heavy bag training and sparring. I didn't get too in-
depth with the movements. Even when doing a strange

movement that didn't make sense, I didn't ask questions, I just mimicked the movement the best I could and moved on.

I've trained many of the major form sets of Taekwondo. The taeguk forms of World Taekwondo Federation (WTF), the songham forms of the American Taekwondo Association (ATA), and the original International Taekwondo Federation (ITF) forms, and that's just Taekwondo. Throw in weapons forms as well as random forms I've learned from other arts and my rolodex at one point was around sixty forms rolling around my head. For those under thirty, a rolodex is like a physical version of your contacts list on your smartphone, but with less legibility and more coffee stains. Sixty forms I put almost no effort into understanding. It wasn't until well into my black belt ranks that I began to dig deeper into the forms I knew and started discovering the brilliance behind both the techniques and the form as a whole. Once I saw the forms on a deeper level, my performance of them increased as did my entire training regimen in all of the martial arts styles I practiced. I saw a noticeable step up in power and balance in all of my movements as well as footwork for arts like Hapkido that are geared towards grappling and don't use forms.

Forms, Kata, Patterns, Poomse, it goes by many names, but in many cases, students dislike them. It's understandable. There's no bag to hit. There's no one to spar. There are no boards to break. Generally speaking, they are bland at first look. Many schools over the years have removed forms training stating that it's not realistic, or they are boring. This is likewise understandable, as what they say is true. It is boring and not noticeably realistic for many. This makes it difficult to retain students.

For those that don't know what forms training is, it's a sequence of martial arts moves linked together (typically from eighteen to eighty moves) simulating a fight sequence but with just yourself punching the air. However, just because it's not realistic by itself, doesn't mean it's not useful. Just because it's boring at first look, doesn't mean you won't develop an appreciation for it once you've fully understood their purpose.

What is the purpose? Forms training is an integral part of any martial arts that wants to develop balance, power in kicking/striking, and control. There are many different ways to make use of forms training. For my Taekwondo students, the emphasis is on power. Each technique is meant to be done with one hundred percent power, nothing less. With this power training, control, balance, and proper body alignment are developed greatly.

As I explain it to my students, forms training teaches you 100% power, balance, control, and footwork. One step sparring (pre-determined sparring) teaches you speed, accuracy and distancing. Then, you put them together for sparring. This isn't the only way to make use of forms however, this is just what I currently teach my students. Not only does it change from school to school, it may change over time. Everyone grows and learns, instructors included. In ten years' time, I may use my forms in a completely different way. It doesn't make them better, just different.

Many forms have movements in them that to the outside looking in, make no sense. Not all techniques are just kicks, strikes, or blocks. Some are self-defense movements such as a grab or sweep. In order to perform the form correctly, one must fully understand every technique in the form.

There is yet another element to many traditional forms that is heavily overlooked. That is the meaning behind the form and why it was created. For instance, look at some of the original Taekwondo black belt forms such as GeBaek, a form named after a strict general in the Korean Army. The form is done in straight line and with extreme power and control and balance, not a lot of fancy techniques. This represents GeBaek's strict, powerful, and straight forward leadership. With this in mind while doing this form, one should be very strict with their movements, no wasted movements, nothing fancy or off balance, but very grounded and powerful.

Even newer forms created today have reasoning behind them, or they should. While some forms are done strictly for competition purposes to look fancy and give the competitor high scores, the more traditional way of doing forms helps train a student in specific skills and movements that will be used in sparring. Many traditional forms represent specific elements. A fire form should be done with passion and desire. A water form should flow naturally and smoothly with no resistance.

There are potentially millions of forms out there throughout the martial arts universe, and more are being created today, but nearly all have a meaning behind them. Once you find that meaning, then and only then, will you do the form correctly and learn what was meant to be taught by doing that form.

With all of this said, not all martial arts styles and schools need forms. My Hapkido program doesn't make use of forms, other than a couple of weapons forms at the black belt level. That doesn't mean one program is better than the other, every style and system is different. Some styles need forms, others don't. I do find though that styles that make use of forms result in students with more power and balance than those styles that don't have them. Then again, some styles don't need all of those elements to be successful.

While you may not love forms, I hope you understand how incredibly useful they can be and that they are designed to help you with self-defense. You have to learn the alphabet before you learn to write a novel. It may take considerable time, but the end result will be much greater.

CHAPTER 6

Let Odin take the wheel

Students after a knife defense seminar. In order from left to right: Enmanual Tejada, Kevin Moldoch, Antje Almeida, Paulo Almeida, David Girardot. Photo by Dan Bourelle

The mugger jumps out of nowhere, demanding your wallet and threatening you and your date. You, in turn, jump into action! You will not be a victim today! You knock the knife out of his hand. You rifle off a couple of combinations to the mugger's head and abdomen. You then follow it up by throwing him to the ground with a perfectly executed hip toss and taking his knife. You've protected yourself and made your date beam with excitement over you, her new hero!

Okay, stop day dreaming, here's what's really going to happen. You're going to attempt to knock the knife out of his hand, but end up cutting yourself. You'll attempt a combination of kicks and strikes. Sadly, you will have forgotten all of your technique and revert back to your patented wild right hook repeated over and over. You'll miss more times than not. You'll then go in to throw him, you'll make a mistake like you've done in class multiple times and will stop in the middle of it to correct the technique, just like in class. At that time, the mugger will grab your wallet and attempt to run, only to be dropped by your date who just pepper-sprayed him. Smooth as broken glass my friend!

Back in the late nineties, I had placed a lot of effort into point sparring competitions. I believe I was a green belt in Taekwondo and close to attaining my black belt in Hapkido. My instructor was a law enforcement officer and with the S.W.A.T. team in my home town. We had obtained what we dubbed, "The Gorilla Suit." It was the latest in technology, full body protective suit. It was considered indestructible and the material was unable to be torn or cut with a knife. This thing was AMAZING!!!

My brother, my instructor and I watched a video of it being tested. People whaling on each other with bats, batons, knives and even showing old versions of the suit being hit by cars and attacked by bears. This was ours to play, err, train with! Like any new toy, we put it on and beat the snot out of each other as we giggled with enthusiasm.

The next class, we brought out the suit for training. My instructor suited up and we went through a scenario of an attacker (my instructor) would charge in at you however he wants to. Our goal is to drop him to the ground as fast as possible. He demonstrated how to use low kicks to set up strikes and elbows to the head before sweeping to the ground, among other options. After he went through each student, it was my turn to unleash the beast!

He charged after me to take me down. I, with my unstoppable Taekwondo kicks which I used to rack up the points at competitions all around the region, sprang into action. I pivoted and threw out an amazing round kick to his head with all I had!

He stopped, looked at me with confusion, and asked, "What was that?" His head didn't even move slightly from my kick, let alone get dropped by it.

"Hit me hard!" he reminded me.

We reset and did it again. I swung that round kick out as hard as I possibly could! *Tink.* No effect. My instructor stopped and told me I need to stop training for point sparring competitions for a while and we adjusted my defense for something other than kicks.

What happened here? Was I just incredibly weak and unable to produce any power to drop him? Nope, I had quite a bit of power actually. The problem was just what my instructor mentioned. I was training too much for point sparring competitions. In point sparring, power doesn't mean anything. It's basically a game of tag using kicks and strikes. It's actually in the competitors favor not to hit too hard, which would waste energy. I had trained myself out of hitting hard during sparring.

I could smash boards and destroy pads and heavy bags, but that wasn't sparring or self-defense. That's like doing a lot of pushups or bench pressing to have a stronger punch, but never practicing your punch. No matter how strong you get, that punch will be laughable. My trained, instinctual reaction was to kick lightly for a point. That was a huge wakeup call in my training.

I made some critical changes to my training in order to overcome that issue. For instance, when throwing a round kick in point sparring, you point your knee at the target and then extend the lower leg to make contact. If you point right at the target, you'll never hit too hard. However, if you point that knee a few inches through that target, you'll smash it! It took me a considerable amount of time to make those adjustments to hit hard during sparring in order to be ready for my black belt testing.

When, or if, the time comes that we need to put our martial arts skills into action, we will go into autopilot and perform the way we train.

We don't rise to the level of our expectations – we fall to the level of our training – Archilochus.

You have to ask yourself, how well do you train? Do you train properly? We all make, or have made, mistakes in our training. I want to give you a short do and don't list that can help you perform as efficiently as possible if that time comes, but first, let me explain the whys.

Our state of mind is dramatically different when confronted with a stressful situation. Our body is under control by a completely different system behind the wheel. During day to day life and normal activities, our body makes use of the parasympathetic nervous system or PNS. This system takes care of daily activities that make use of cognitive processing and fine or complex motor skills.

Think of it like this. Our security team is just sitting back watching the monitors as the janitors and maintenance crew do their jobs to keep the place working properly. When a stressful situation hits however, such as our life being threatened, the sympathetic nervous system (SNS) takes over. This is also known as the "fight or flight system," or as I prefer to call it, the "fight, flight, or freeze system."

Think of this one as the alarms in the building have gone off and the security team has been sent out into action as the janitors and maintenance crew run and hide. Many bodily functions cease when the SNS is in control. This includes digestion, fine and complex motor skills, and even cognitive thought processing. You're essentially left with instincts and training.

If your training consists of casually going through movements, or only doing parts of the technique and not completing the action since it's "inconvenient" during class, then guess what? You'll do the exact same thing when the time comes to use that technique. If you train by taking your partner down but not finishing them, or controlling them, and then help them back up, you will do the exact same thing in the street. You will take them down, then you will offer your hand out to help them up, then they say thanks as they begin to pummel you and finish their objective.

Stories of ridiculous mistakes such as this run rampant in law enforcement due to poor training methods. Such as the officer who wrestled a gun away from a perpetrator with excellent technique, only to hand the gun right back to him to be shot. Why? Because that's the way he trained. Every time he practiced disarming during training, he would hand the gun back to his partner so he could practice again. It became instinctive.

You may ask, "How could he possibly think giving the gun back to the perpetrator is a good idea?" The answer is, there was no thought. That part of the brain is not always functioning during a life-threatening moment like that, only instincts are in control.

With all of that said, how do we train ourselves so that our autopilots are trained properly? Let's get started with some smart tips.

The Do list:

Do train in the gym as you would perform in the street. Make sure you follow through with your techniques. When doing a takedown, make sure you follow it up completely to a position where you are in full control and/or have made your partner tap out. Release the pressure, but continue to hold the position for a moment more before jumping back up. Do this on a regular basis but not all the time. Understand that sometimes the situation calls for a quick drop of the opponent then on to the next opponent.

Do practice full force on a regular basis when it comes to strikes/kicks. This can simply be on a heavy bag or on a well-padded partner, but it's imperative to do so. If you practice pulling your punches so you don't hurt your partner all the time, then you will do the same in the street.

Do know your limits and weaknesses. Then strengthen or learn to protect them as they will be targeted in a real altercation. Let go of your ego and practice the stuff you are not good at. Ignoring it can lead to the loss of your life.

Do spar. It's an absolute must. I've had, and have students that just loathe sparring. Whether it's because they don't feel they are good at it, they think it's too violent, or some other excuse. If your intent is just to have a social hobby, then that's perfectly fine. If your intent is to learn self-defense, then you must spar. It's the closest thing you have to real combat and the only way to fully prepare for something is to do it, or something as close to it as possible. Understand though that limits must be shown. Self-defense is about protecting the body, if you spar so hard that you are injured all the time, it kind of defeats the point, doesn't it?

Be efficient. Many traditional arts are full of long drawn out fancy techniques. There is nothing wrong with these techniques, they have their purpose, but understand they are not always efficient. Concentrate on quick, precise techniques with the highest chance of success.

Do put yourself into stressful situations. Rank testings, tournaments, demos, sparring the biggest and baddest guy in the gym-these are all great ways to truly test and teach yourself how to perform under stress.

The Don't list:

Don't let a failed technique stop you. I see students do this far too often. They initiate a technique, make a mistake and then stop and start over. Don't do this, even if you royally mess up, keep going. Alter the technique if needed, but get your partner to the ground and control him, make it successful. The only exception is if you, or your partner, are in danger of being injured.

Don't be a lazy attacker. This too bugs me when I see a student stand straight up and down, feet next to each other and reaching out holding a choke or a grab of some sort attempting to represent an attacker. No attacker will do this! Grab with intent. Yes, we start easy and relaxed when we first learn the techniques, but once you have learned it, it's time for your attacker to find ways to resist and be stubborn, just like a real attacker in the street.

Don't avoid working with the guy/girl that frustrates you. We all know that student who never turns the right way nor cooperates the way you want. It may be annoying, but this is where the real learning is. Everyone is different in their actions and responses to techniques. You must learn them all to be fully prepared.

Don't be erratic with your training. Dropping in for a month of training and then stopping for three months is not going to work. You need constant ongoing training to both learn and retain those instinctive skill sets.

While this isn't everything it takes to be more efficient and successful with training your self-defense skills, it's a good start. Next time you're in class, just ask yourself, "Is this helping or hurting me in my training?" and you'll have your answer.

CHAPTER 7

The Incline - Located in Manitou Springs, Co. A daunting vertical hike nearly a mile high with over 2700 steps to the top. Photo by Dan Bourelle

The contagiousness of limits

"Bruce had me up to three miles a day, really at a good pace. We'd run the three miles in twenty-one or twenty-two minutes. Just under eight minutes a mile

So, this morning he said to me "We're going to go five."

"Bruce, I can't go five. I'm a helluva lot older than you are, and I can't do five."

"When we get to three, we'll shift gears and it's only two more and you'll do it."

"Okay, hell, I'll go for it."

We get to three, we go into the fourth mile and I'm okay for three or four minutes, and then I really begin to give out.

I'm tired, my heart's pounding, I can't go any more.

"Bruce if I run anymore," — and we're still running — "if I run any more I'm liable to have a heart attack and die."

"Then die."

It made me so mad that I went the full five miles.

Afterward I went to the shower and then I wanted to talk to him about it.

I said, you know, "Why did you say that?"

"Because you might as well be dead. Seriously, if you always put limits on what you can do, physical or anything else, it'll spread over into the rest of your life. It'll spread into your work, into your morality, into your entire being. There are no limits. There are plateaus, but you must not stay there, you must go beyond them. If it kills you, it kills you. A man must constantly exceed his level."

- The Art of Expressing the Human Body
by John Little

We're told our entire lives what we can and can't do. What's right and what's wrong. Boundaries and limits are listed in every aspect of our lives. Most are to keep order and peace, but some are created in our own mind. Whether it's based on previous experience, fear, or on what someone we trust has told us, we have limits everywhere.

Let's do an experiment. Go to your kitchen and take out some bread, deli meat, cheese, and pickles. Now make yourself a sandwich. Okay, you can just imagine doing this; you don't actually have to if you aren't hungry or don't like sandwiches. Now, did you take two pieces of bread, open them up, place the meat on first, then the cheese, then the pickles? Maybe some of you didn't, but I'm guessing most of you did exactly that. Why? Is there a rule that says you have to make the sandwich in that order? Does the cheese being on the meat and under the pickles create some sort of super flavor compared to any other order? And why did you open the bread? Is there a top and bottom? And do you always start eating it from the same side? The rounded side first, am I right?

It's quite strange what we place rules and limits on. Maybe it helps keep order in our mind, or maybe we were shown a way to do things when we first learned and have simply done things the same way ever since. I'm sure there are many different answers, but the fact remains that we really don't need these limits and rules. Sometimes they mean nothing, and sometimes they hold us back or waste our time.

It's true what Bruce Lee stated in the quote at the onset of this chapter. If we limit ourselves in one aspect of our life, it will bleed over into other aspects. I see this constantly in the martial arts. "I can't do that." "That's too complicated." "My body doesn't move like that." It's no surprise that many of these students end up quitting or constantly hold themselves back from reaching the next level.

I've seen a 400 pound man do a jump spin crescent kick with the grace of a swan and the striking speed of a cobra. If you don't know what that kick is, look it up on YouTube and then rethink your own limits. Don't tell me your 130 pound injury free body can't do it.

I've even had numerous people tell me they aren't in good enough shape to do martial arts, and want to wait until they are in better shape to start. Let's look past the fact that martial arts can help you get into shape and does not require one to be in shape. The fact is that of those people that have told me they aren't in shape enough, none have come back to me in shape and ready to start. That's because they placed a limit on themselves by saying they weren't in shape enough to do martial arts.

Do you really think those limits stopped right there?

Nope, they weren't in shape enough to get a gym membership or go running either I'm sure. Possibly too busy to find time to do what little they think they can do. I'll teach occasional women's self-defense seminars and will ask various women to come take the class. Guess which ones find reasons not to take the class? The outgoing, confident personalities that are the least likely to be attacked? Nope, it's the ones who need it the most. The ones who tell themselves they aren't physically capable of defending themselves and are easily discouraged in doing anything that can build their confidence, leading to being the most victimized person around. These limits we place on ourselves constantly bleed over into other aspects of our lives. However, removing limits in one aspect in life has the same effect; you begin to remove limits in other aspects of your life as well. Start small if you have to.

Limits aren't all bad though. I'm not just talking about societies rules and limits either. We need mental limits as well. Without them, we lose objectives to reach for. For instance, when I was younger I used to love to draw and was quite good at it. However, if you gave me a pencil and paper and told me to draw anything I like, you'd be more likely to see a paper airplane flying around your head than my next drawing masterpiece.

However, tell me to draw something as boring as a cow and I'd get right on it. Yet it'd never be the cow you thought you were going to get. Maybe a Rambo-fied cow with guns and knives shooting down helicopters or possibly just an extremely overweight man stewing in his own filth. But never just a cow. I was very creative, but needed limits and boundaries for me to push and manipulate. Give me no limits and I had no direction, nothing to attain. Tell me I can't do something and watch it be done. Those limits were meant to be exceeded, just simply mile markers on the road to something bigger.

Even when we are told there are no rules, we seem to have unspoken rules. A fear of being rude. A fear of being disrespectful or not doing what you thought you were told. We tend to live in a box full of unspoken rules. I find this a lot when explaining movements and ideas and situations to students. I'll give a pretty simple command with little to no rules behind it, yet watch as the students set up their own limits and rules to complete the action.

For instance, I'll tell multiple students to attack one student for sparring. I may even say, "Don't take turns and just go after him." And yet, they still attack one at a time, being mindful not to get in the way of the defender doing a defense. It usually takes multiple explanations and adjustments to get them to remove the unspoken "courtesy" from their sparring.

Even then, some will go half speed, some will go full speed but then allow the defender to take them down and control them with no resistance. Some will lightly tap each other and fall in the direction they think they are supposed to fall. Where did these rules come from? Essentially, its etiquette, courtesy, and respect for their partners. It's an attempt to help each other be successful and not get injured. Yet this practice will only lead to failure and injury in a real self-defense situation. Now suddenly these mental limits are potentially leading to life ending mistakes in real confrontations. Yes, it's important to have common sense and not drop the smallest guy on his head and then break his arm, but no, it's not okay to let the smaller or lower rank student think he's successful all the time. These limits are now hurting both of you.

It's a complicated matter. We worry that we are over stepping our boundaries (or others' boundaries) and we hold back knowing that it's safer to hold back than over shoot. My answer to that is, don't be afraid to ask questions. More times than not, I want my students doing more, not less, and trying to push those boundaries, not be restricted by them.

Author Rory Miller gives a great description of this in his book, *Meditations on Violence.* I won't list everything he has written as I want you to go read his book(s), but I want to point out a couple of his "permissions" as it pertains to this chapter of limits:

You have permission to beat me, even if I wear a blackbelt. You have permission to become better than the best instructor you ever had.

In my past life I worked in the Architectural and Engineering world as a CAD (computer aided design) detailer. Essentially, I used the computer to draw buildings, among other things, for people to build from. I first got into this profession during junior high school. One of my drafting instructors in high school said something the first day of class that has stuck with me ever since.

He stated, "My goal this year is to get you to know more about, and be better than me at AutoCAD®" (a computer program we used to draw with).

Everyone in class laughed as he was not only incredible at this program, but how could anyone be better than the person who taught them? That was what we all thought. By the end of the school year, many students had played around with the program enough to show him new things he had not known about. He succeeded.

Because of his success, I had a pretty easy time in college and actually knew more about the program than the instructors, which led to getting my first job offer before I even graduated college. I now tell my students the same thing my drafting teacher told me. "You will be a better first degree black belt than I was and better than I was at every single rank."

Much like myself and the other students in that drafting class years ago, my students laugh and don't believe me. The fact is, every single student I've promoted to black belt has been better than I was on many levels. They know more about the art. They know more about the material. They understand more about what's expected of them. I've been quite successful at creating better black belts than myself.

We were once told that humans can't fly. The Wright brothers changed that. Touching the stars was once unattainable. Then we set foot on the moon. For years it was considered scientifically impossible to run a mile under four minutes. Many got near that four minute mark but never beat it. Until one day it was beaten, nowadays it's common. It wasn't their bodies holding them back, nor their training, it was their mind telling them it wasn't possible.

Those who achieve the impossible have left major marks and ripples throughout history. They set new imaginary lines in the sand, not to show where the edge of possible and impossible lay, but to show what mile marker they reached and where you need to beat. They all refused to believe that something was impossible. Even those who may not have succeeded have gone down in history as legends just by attempting the impossible. Remember the Alamo? Don't let your limits hold you back as they will certainly bleed over into all aspects of your life, let your limits drive and motivate you to the next level!

"If be possible, it is done. If impossible, it will be done."

— Charles Alexandre de Calonne

Dan successfully reaching the top of the Incline

CHAPTER 8

Standing naked wearing nothing but a black belt

Presenting two of his students their black belts in Moo Hahn Hahn Hapkido after eight years of hard training. Paulo Almeida (left), Dan (middle), Antje Almeida (right).

What is a black belt? And what is needed to attain one? This isn't a simple answer. First, every school and every martial arts style may have different answers to that question. Second, every student is different and therefore every black belt is different and what is needed to attain that black belt is different. But I'll do my best to give you an idea of what it takes in my school.

When they asked Michelangelo how he made his statue of David he said, "It is easy. You just chip away the stone that doesn't look like David."

He was also quoted as saying, "I saw an angel in the block of marble and I just chiseled 'til I set him free."

Many students come to me for multiple reasons. Generally speaking, it's to learn a skill such as self-defense or body control. While martial arts does provide these, its greatest attribute is a journey of self-discovery. Look around any martial arts school and you'll find multiple types of people doing multiple different things at multiple different skill levels. All could be the exact same rank. If all we did was taught you a skill, wouldn't everyone be doing the same thing and at the same skill level as others of their rank?

When I first walked into that martial arts studio back in my home town of Norfolk, Nebraska, I had assumed that I was just going to physically add some things to my skill set and add another notch to my belt of physical accomplishments. After a few embarrassing moments that showed me I wasn't as good as I thought, I began my journey of self-discovery. Decades later, that journey is still going strong and the discoveries have only increased over time. For many, martial arts begins as a physical attainment. Yet, for anyone who sticks around and puts any effort into it, they'll discover that the biggest gains aren't from physical attainment, but from self-realizations. You will discover physical and mental limitations as well as strengths and weaknesses you never knew were there.

Why is self-awareness and the realization of your own strengths and weakness so important to self-defense? In some ways it's obvious, when you know your weaknesses you can work to strengthen them or at least protect them. Then, when you learn what your strengths are, you can cater your skills around it. There is also another reason.

As much as we like to believe that the people who we seek defense from are nothing like us, the fact is, they are a lot like us. The school bullies, the thieves looking for your wallet, the drunken college student who thinks you looked at his girl wrong, the rapist, and even the serial killer, they aren't monsters from another planet, they are us. They have the same needs, the same emotions, the same desires, the same feelings, the same strengths, and the same weaknesses. We are all capable of both doing good things and doing bad things. The only difference is our perspective and perceived justification for what we are doing.

When you truly understand who you are, what you are capable of, and why you do what you do, you will better understand those evildoers. You will understand why they want to hurt you, how they will hurt you, and even when they will hurt you. If you know this information, then you can avoid issues altogether. This is the highest attainment of self-defense.

Defending yourself without physically having to defend yourself is where it's at. Pardon me as I take a side step from this chapter to make something very clear. Violence isn't what most think it is, neither are fights. It's not like it is on TV. The reality of fighting involves not just temporary physical damage, but psychological damage that may last forever, not to mention the possibilities of contracting diseases. Did you think that fight wasn't going to be bloody? Do you think that person physically attacking you has kept themselves clean? Do you think you will ever walk down that sidewalk again without flashbacks of what happened? No, avoidance is the only way to purely defend yourself with no consequences, all other roads lead to lasting problems. Now back to the topic at hand.

Most of my students, as they get closer and closer to earning their black belt, ask me the same question. Generally, the question is along these lines, "What do I need to do to earn my black belt?" They all know the physical movements and expectations I have of them, but most realize over time that physical skill is not enough to please me or to earn a black belt. I never have a great general answer for them as the specific answer changes from student to student, but one portion of the answer that tends to include everyone is "failure."

No, I don't tell them they are going to fail. Though some of the greatest self-discoveries come from failure. I set my students up for success, yes, but then I also set an impossible task in front of them in order to fail. It's not about the failure, though, it's about what they do with it. When you realize that you aren't as strong as you thought you were, or that the skills you thought were perfect during class suddenly dissolve when your body and mind are exhausted. When your endless endurance finally hits the wall. When your ego gets thrown to the floor and stomped on when all eyes are on you. It's what you do next that determines who you really are.

Antje Almeida and Paulo Almeida shortly after their black belt testing.
Photo by Dan Bourelle

The stone has been chipped away, the only thing left standing is your naked self for all to see. With your imperfections exposed and highlighted. Do you give up? Do you run and hide? Do you deny what just happened? Or do you accept your failures, discover who you really are and stand with pride of this discovery and knowledge of yourself? If you choose the latter, then your black belt awaits. It will not be given to you; you will take it, as it was never mine. I was just holding it for you until you realized it was yours the whole time and that you now truly feel worthy of wearing it.

Understand though that black belt is not the end, it's the true beginning. Everything leading up to it was just preparing you for the real journey. It was the chipping away of the biggest slabs of stone. I learned more as a first degree going to a second degree than all the years spent as a colored belt. I learned more as a second degree going for my third degree than I have all the years spent getting to second degree. This, at least so far, has continued to be the case as I stand here working towards my seventh degree. Each passing year I look back at what I knew a year ago, both about martial arts and myself, and have thought to myself, "Wow, how little did I know a year ago?!" I see no end, nor even slowing, in sight. For every new door of knowledge and self-discovery I open, ten more doors await for me on the other side.

The martial arts belt around your waist is not there for looks. It's not there to keep your pants up. It has no special powers. It does not guarantee you success, nor does it guarantee you respect or courtesy from others. It simply reflects the wearer's knowledge of self-realization and their knowledge of the martial arts.

The white belt you wear on day one reflects the fact that you know nothing of the martial arts and may truly know nothing about yourself. The more elements of knowledge you gain along the way the darker the belt becomes. From oranges and yellows to purples and blues and browns. Constantly chipping way that stone that isn't you, until finally, your true self is exposed and you know yourself. That massive amount of knowledge is then reflected through your belt as the darkest color possible, black. There is an angel inside that block of stone around you; will you hide it from the world, or will you chisel your way out?

CHAPTER 9

Success isn't won in the lottery

Dan being awarded the men's instructor of the year award by Hanshi Larry Isaac during a martial arts banquet in Myrtle Beach, SC

"I hope all this bad luck stops soon."

"I pray things get better for me."

"I wish this was all easier."

Any of these statements sound familiar? Maybe they, or something similar, have been uttered by you even today? It's normal, we all hope for things to be easier or to be better. Do we really want that, though? If you spent your whole life being rewarded with everything you wanted and never had to work hard or live through adversity and tough times, would you really appreciate it? Of course not.

It's the tough and difficult times that make us appreciate the good times and help develop our character. And it's the end of a good thing that makes you want to make the most of it. Many times we find ourselves pushing and grinding through a bad day wishing things would get better, yet not changing anything we are doing. That's the definition of insanity, doing the same thing over and over and expecting a different result.

It's tough to do, but we have to start making changes. The problem is, what we want is the big stuff, and the big stuff is daunting, seemingly too much for us to do. So instead, we take the comfortable route of doing nothing at all and spending our day wishing and hoping things change on their own. We're accustomed to it, even if we don't like it.

This is one of the many reasons domestic abuse victims stay with their abuser. The fear of change and uncertainty is greater than the fear of the abuse, since they've already experienced the abuse. Ever heard of the saying, "The devil you know is better than the devil you don't know?" What we need to understand is to make the small changes first. A body in motion stays in motion, a body at rest, stays at rest. Any motion at all can have a snowball effect and those little changes can turn into big changes.

Over the years I've watched, participated in, and judged many martial arts rank testings. Some were quite boring and even the students that passed seemed underwhelmed and unexcited to receive their new belt. These students usually didn't have to work hard at it, they put just enough effort into it to pass the bare minimum requirements. Most of these students end up leaving and gaining virtually nothing from the experience. Some even stay long enough to make it to black belt, but then quickly quit afterwards. It was just another notch in the belt for them.

Other rank testings, though, were quite inspiring to watch and judge or even participate in. These students were different. For many, they had failed at previous attempts to gain rank. For others, it was working day after day on a technique that they just couldn't seem to get, until testing. For some it was doing something they never thought possible. Others still, specifically those going for their black belt, it was their going through the gauntlet that is the black belt testing.

Being exhausted in every ounce of their body and being knocked down over and over. Knocked down to the point where a normal person would have been broken, only to realize they are still standing. Knowing that each time they stood back up, each small step forward and every second they stand there not giving up, is a small victory headed towards a larger victory. That victory being their black belt, which in turn can be a small step towards another victory, a transformation of self.

These are the moments we yearn for as martial artists. Standing there at the end of it all looking back at the hell you went through and knowing that if you've done it once, you can do it again, and again, and again. Everything else seems easy now. It's always worth it when you finally taste success. One success will lead to others, and soon your lofty goals when you started are being realized.

Be driven by something bigger than yourself.

Ask a person to fight for themselves and you may get limited effort, if any at all. On the counter, ask someone to fight for their child, loved one, or something they believe in and watch them do things you never thought possible. It's engrained in us to do so. It's how our species, and all species that live in groups, survived throughout history. We fight for the greater good of our species, even if it means sacrificing our own comfort or even lives.

I've noticed something over the years. Those who have something bigger than themselves to fight for tend to be more successful in accomplishing their goals. It doesn't really matter what that something is, we just tend to fight harder for everything but ourselves and when we feel others depend on us to get the job done.

I fight for my students and clients' success. I truly believe that I can have an impact on creating a better society, even if it's through my students, or students of students, years down the road. It's what drives me to do what I do everyday. To push through the difficult times and why I've consistently ignored those who have said I can't win the battle I'm fighting.

I'm reminded of a great poem I came across years ago titled, *The Final Inspection* by Sgt. Joshua Helterbran. The poem is about a military soldier, upon death, standing in front of his god waiting for judgment. It states that he sacrificed his entire life helping calm and protect others, and therefore he wasn't always able to be a saint or spend much time at church. The poem concludes with his god stating, *Walk peacefully on Heaven's streets, You've done your time in Hell.*

This poem may have been geared towards a military soldier, but to me, it's about all warriors. Warriors don't just fight with guns on a battle field. Some warriors fight as teachers, others as parents, others still as volunteers. At the end of the day, it's all for the same thing, the greater good and helping others become successful or live more fulfilling and free lives. Everyone finds their "something bigger" in different places, and can experience or create their own personal heaven and hell right here on earth.

A mother, still in her prime, stricken with cancer had to make a decision. A decision to take the cancer treatments that could extend her life briefly but leave her horribly ill, or pass away sooner without the additional pain and suffering. She had sworn all her life she would never take chemo. She believed it wasn't worth it just to stay alive in that condition and that the pain and sickness wasn't worth the extended life. When the doctors said it would only add a few weeks to her life, it should have been an easy answer. Yet, she decided to take the treatment that would prolong the agony of the disease. Why? Because she was a mother of three, and in particular, a six-year-old boy whose only world was his mother.

She needed more time to teach him as much as she could before she left this world and left him on his own - not just to survive, but to thrive, and possibly even do something great with his life. She may not have had a plan on how to go about teaching him these things, or even if he'd remember what she did for him, but she had to try.

You may have guessed it, but that was my mother, and that six-year-old child was me. My memory of that time is quite foggy and distorted, and I don't know what she taught me during that time, but it doesn't matter. What she did to spend that extra time with me was all that was needed to teach me something special. What we think we are capable of in life is just a fraction of what we really are capable of when we have something to fight for that is greater than us. I urge you to find that something, and to fight for it to enrich your life and the lives around you.

Dan with his mother, Shirley Bourelle in one of their last photos together.

CHAPTER 10

Broken parts and missing pieces

I can still hear the electronic tune playing in my head from throwing a strike on my 1981 Coleco Bowlatronic™ handheld bowling game. There were some missing parts. The battery holder flap was missing and you had to hold the battery in a very specific spot to make the game work. Careful not to sneeze or the game would reset! I believe there was a light or two burned out. Yet, I played the that game until my thumbs were numb and my eyes blood shot.

My old 1940s miniature pool table made with a metal frame, chalk board-like top, mini wooden pool cue sticks and clay pool balls, was a little worse for wear. The table became unattached and had to be glued back in place the best we could. We lost one stick. We lost a few of the pool balls so we replaced them with marbles that weren't quite the same size or weight. Yet, I didn't care as I pressed on to be a mini pool master!

I could go on and on with examples of broken toys as most of my toys were hand me downs from my father, brothers, and cousins or bought for twenty five cents at a local garage sale. Most of these toys had broken parts and missing pieces, but I didn't care. I loved them. Even today most of the equipment at my studio was donated or bought from second hand stores and websites and are missing pieces. Some of my standing heavy bags no longer stand, others are stuck on the lowest height.

Even at my home much of my stuff is a bit worse for wear. My computer that I'm typing this on stops me every hour to pop up a screen asking me to type in a number to authenticate my Windows program that came with the computer, yet I have no number. I just click through and cancel out and resume my writing, only to have it pop up again an hour later. I'm guessing most people are in the same boat. A phone that doesn't run an app properly or has a cracked screen. A car that constantly has the check engine light on because it's too expensive to fix. A favorite coffee mug that has a crack in it. A grill in which the ignition button no longer works so you just throw numerous matches in there trying to light it making sure you stay at a distance as when it lights, it all but explodes in flames for a moment. Now that I'm typing that out, maybe I should invest in a less deadly grill.

Anyway, most of these are normal things. We don't get that bothered by things that aren't in perfect condition. We expect things to slowly break or lose a piece and just plow through with using them until they completely break. This begs the question, why is it when we have a stubbed toe that we cancel all plans to go to the gym or martial arts classes? We have this tendency to only attend these things if we are in perfect condition.

I've heard all of the excuses over the years. "I'm not in good enough shape yet to do martial arts, let me get fit first." "I'm under a lot of stress right now in my life, let me deal with that first before doing classes." "I'm not talented enough to learn martial arts." "I'm too old for martial arts." "My ankle is a bit sore, let me rest it tonight and return to class next week." "The universe hasn't shown me a sign yet to begin classes." All ridiculous excuses that I hear regularly.

Martial arts doesn't care about any of these things, nor should you. Those who are out of shape, under stress, untalented, or too old, are the ones who get the most out of martial arts. If taught and trained correctly, it will make you more physically fit, reduce stress, develop skill, and help ward off the effects of aging. You know the person who gets the least out of martial arts classes? The physically fit, talented, confident young person who usually just adds their black belt to their overloaded trophy case. While I enjoy having those talented students, they're about one percent of the students I get and most typically stick around for a short amount of time before moving on to the next adventure.

The students who tend to fill my classes are the ones that feared joining the most, believing they weren't good enough or would do poorly. Those are the students that tend to dramatically improve their lives and overcome obstacles in their lives.

Have a sore shoulder, broken foot or some other injury? Use that to be a better martial artist! The assumption is that we can't do our normal material when we have an injury, so we must halt our training. No! Martial arts is about self-defense. Do you think an attacker is going to hold off on attacking you just because you have a sling on or a cast on your foot or because you have a headache? No! Training when you are "broken" is absolutely crucial.

You have to learn to get around injuries, headaches, and stress when learning self-defense or you'll be useless if you ever have to use your training in a realistic situation. People don't get attacked when they are most ready to be attacked. They are attacked when they least expect it and are least prepared for it. Watch nature videos sometime and tell me which zebra gets eaten. The young, strong, healthy zebra that runs faster than the rest of the pack? Or the one that has a broken leg? Maybe if that zebra would have taken the time to train with me while injured, it wouldn't have gotten eaten, just saying.

Winston Churchill, Dan's English bulldog. Pre and post spinal tumor.

Around 2016, my English Bulldog, Winston Churchill, was diagnosed with a tumor on this spinal cord after I noticed his hind leg acting wonky as he walked. The amount of effort that would be needed to help keep him going (meds, wheelchair, extra hygiene care, etc.) on the part of my me and my brother as well as the amount of effort needed on Winston's part to stay motivated to keep moving, was daunting. Neither we, nor the doctors, were optimistic about his life expectancy. We decided, though, that Winston's time will be up when he decides it will be up.

To everyone's surprise, Winston plugged away like a champ for years after his diagnoses. He would even grumble at me if I tried to carry him up the stairs early on. He demanded to do it himself with me just lightly lifting his hind legs so they didn't drag. Over time, he eventually allowed me to carry him when needed. He cheerfully took to the streets with his wheelchair to go on walks around the neighborhood. Every neighbor knew him by name and came out to give him snacks and pet him as we proudly trotted around the loop. I was somewhat jealous as these same people never knew my name, and only occasionally addressed me. I clearly was never the star of this show.

Even without his wheelchair, he roamed the house and back yard, hind legs dragging behind, not letting anything slow him down! He was a fighter! Winston was inspiring to all that knew him. His personality wasn't paralyzed, only his hind legs. Point being, Winston found ways to do his daily routine, despite the tragic diagnoses. Sadly, after about three years of no issues, Winston began having seizures that we believed were caused by one of the meds he was on. We switched meds, but this then led to other issues such as vomiting and lethargy. Between the seizures that wouldn't stop, growing pain, and vomiting all day and night, Winston finally decided it was time to move on.

When he stopped eating and refused to go on a walk to see the neighbors, I knew it was time. He had stopped fighting. I've learned a lot from Winston over the decade I was blessed to have him in my life. His fighting spirit and willingness to smile and love everyone while making adjustments to deal with things that were out of his control was one of the biggest lessons he taught me. More people need to be like Winston!

Winston in his wheelchair while out on a walk.

With all of this said, there is one time you should never go to class and train. That is when you have a contagious illness. No one wants to have what you have, so stay away. Beyond that, however, make it to class! Stop finding reasons to not go to class or to the gym, start looking for reasons to go.

There is a great quote by Reid Hoffman, the founder of LinkedIn™, "If you are not embarrassed by the first version of your product, you've launched too late." In a way, this fits this article well. If you wait for the stars to align and to feel perfect and ready for training, then you've waited too long, and will most likely be waiting forever. We are all full of broken pieces and are missing parts. That's what makes us unique and interesting. We must accept this and deal with it rather than pushing off all the important elements of life until we are fixed. It's not going to happen. We weren't meant to be fully fixed, only improved. We were meant to figure out how to deal with our brokenness, not wait for it to go away before starting the race!

CHAPTER 11

Easy as breathing

Dan's youth students working on their breathing exercises before class starts.
Photo by Dan Bourelle

Breathe in, breathe out, breathe in, breathe out. How awful would it be if we had to consciously think about our breathing? Have you ever thought about your breathing? Don't think too hard, you may pass out! Luckily, we don't have to think about breathing in order for it to happen. Our autonomic nervous system takes care of this, as well as many other bodily functions such as heart rate, digestion, adrenaline dumps, tunnel vision, vasoconstriction of the blood vessels, and so on and so forth.

Recall back to Chapter 6 when I mentioned the SNS system. This is under the umbrella of the autonomic nervous system or involuntary actions. I'll make mention of it numerous times as it's an extremely important system to understand when it relates to self-defense. For brevity, I'll give bits and pieces of the system as they relate to the topic at hand rather than dump a long winded science lesson on you!

The conscious or voluntary stuff is part of the somatic nervous system. Movement of body limbs fall under this somatic category. When fear strikes, the autonomic nervous system (specifically the SNS - sympathetic nervous system) kicks in when the heart rate goes up suddenly. Depending on how high the heart rate goes, this could have a positive effect on your performance (increased vision, hearing and motor skills around one hundred beats per minute) or it could have a negative effect (tunnel vision, muted hearing and decreased motor function over two hundred beats per minute.) We can't directly control these autonomic effects.

What if I told you that there was an indirect way we could control the autonomic effects, and that in a matter of seconds you could raise your heart rate into the perfect level to create the benefits? Or in that same amount of time you could drop an elevated heart rate to ease or even remove those negative effects and put you back into the positive effects? You can. While martial artists for centuries have known how to do this, they've always shrouded it in mystery. I'm here to tell you there is no mystery or mysticism or even that it's that hard to do. It's actually quite simple. As with most everything though, it takes some practice.

In many martial arts tournaments you never know when you are going to compete, you just have to be ready when you're name or division is called. And when it's called, there is very little time to get warmed up, stretched out, and mentally prepared. If it takes you more than a few minutes to reach optimal performance, you're out of luck. I once competed at a tournament where I arrived at seven in the morning and was told to be ready to compete any time after nine in the morning.

I stood around, not eating, not drinking much so I wouldn't have to take as many bathroom breaks (worried I'd miss the call) and staying ready for my name to be called. At six o'clock in the evening my name was finally called. Needless to say, I wasn't ready anymore. I was starving and exhausted and I hadn't even started my competition. However, when it was time to compete, I did fine. Not great, but fine. Considering I had no food and was partially dehydrated, I did quite well. How? By knowing how to breathe and visualize.

Let's do an exercise. In a moment I want you to close your eyes and, not just remember, but relive a moment in your life that stands out the most in a proud, positive and exciting way. Whether it be the day as a child when you stood up to your bully and he backed down, or the day you ran for five touchdowns in a single game (Al Bundy reference anyone?), or maybe the day you pitched that no hitter and hit a homerun to win the game. Any experience that made you feel alive will work. While doing this, take deep breathes in through your nose and out through your mouth. Feel the air enter down deep into your gut, not just shallow chest breathing. Go ahead, close your eyes and relive that experience. I'll wait.

How do you feel? Is your heart pumping? Do you feel motivated? Can you feel that spark in your gut growing into a flame? It's amazing how a few seconds of visualizing and breathing can dramatically alter both your mental outlook and your physical ability. Don't worry if it didn't work extremely well the first time, the more you do it, the better you will get at it. The ability to tune out everything around you is a huge factor in truly reliving those past experiences.

The more you tune out everything, the better you can immerse yourself in that memory and gain that full physical and mental boost it gave the day it actually happened. Another thing that can help? Music. Some like upbeat music, but that's not always the case. Sometimes a song or style of music can help with the visualization and trigger memories and feelings that bring you back to reliving specific moments to conjure up that desired effect of excitement or even bringing you back to a calmer state if needed.

Now you have the elements you need to raise your heart rate and get your mind and body ready for action quickly, but what about when your heart rate is too high and the negative effects are taking hold? Visualization is highly unlikely to work at this point as your body is under a different state of control, it's now being controlled by the autonomic nervous system (specifically the SNS.) Under this control it is primarily instincts, reaction, and training that effect your actions.

Higher brain power such as critical thinking and reliving memories on command are highly inefficient, and in some cases, just not possible. Visualization is probably out. You're left with breathing. You can still consciously control your breathing, albeit extremely difficult if you do not practice doing so. How do you breathe correctly to control your fear and/or anger? There are actually many ways, and everyone is a little different, however, there is a breathing exercise I've used over the years in classes. Before my youth classes begin, all students must sit down on their line up position, cross their legs, keep a good posture, close their eyes and concentrate on their breathing first and foremost.

The process is as follows: Breathe in (through the nose) for three seconds, hold for three seconds, breathe out (through the mouth) for three seconds, hold for three seconds and repeat. As that becomes easier, the students are to try for four seconds, then five seconds, and continue until they reach about eight seconds. Practice this breathing and feel how it changes your heart rate and concentration, make adjustments as necessary and find what count works best for you. This breathing process can be a life saver. The difference between a heart rate over 200 beats per minute in a serious situation versus a heart rate under two hundred beats per minute can be the difference in life or death, or the difference in making a bad decision versus making a good decision. The breathing must be practiced in order to be natural and instinctual at time of sudden conflict, however. One must practice regularly to make this instinctual.

Breathing exercises and meditation is nothing new. Nothing I've stated here is ground breaking new evidence by any stretch of the imagination. Surprisingly, though, I find so few people that do it or understand how to do it. Many students I discuss these exercises with have made the assumption that it involved sitting in an empty, quiet room for endless hours or meditating on a mountain top to achieve nirvana. While you can do that, very few people have the time for it. You can do these breathing exercises any time, for as long or as little as you like. If you want to delve deeper into this simplistic meditation process, I recommend the book *Get Some Headspace, How Mindfulness Can Change Your Life in Ten Minutes a Day,* by Andy Puddicombe.

Whether you need to get pumped up for an event or need to calm your nerves, take the time to breathe and visualize. If you can learn to control your breathing, then you can, to an extent, control your autonomic nervous system. It may seem mystical to be able to control your heart rate, adrenaline dumps, and where the blood in your body is sent to, but it's not, it all starts with your breathing.

CHAPTER 12

What a bird and squirrel taught me

As I sit at a stop light on my way out of the park after a nice run, I look up at the street light and see a large bird perched up on the top of the light post. A smaller bird then swoops down at it, over and over until the larger bird chases it. They continued to swoop and take turns chasing each other playing with one another. I've seen birds do this before, but have never really paid much attention. I found it quite amusing!

As I drove around the corner back to the house, I noticed two squirrels chasing each other around the neighbor's yard and up and down trees. This too amused me. It also made me think. Wild animals spend their lives searching for food, finding mates, taking care of young all while avoiding predators and death that lurks around every corner. Yet they still take time out of their day to play and enjoy life. While it may be that they are just simply playing, I assume the playing actually helps them sharpen their skills in a non-stressful way that will help them survive in the long run, much like the tiger cub that wrestles with its siblings.

While most of us take vacations or live it up on the weekends I find very few of us take breaks in appropriate ways. Take fitness for instance. For those that actually turn fitness into a lifestyle, they tend to forget to take breaks. It's important to take a break from weight training on occasion. A couple weeks break every couple of months is not only helpful, but will allow the body to rest and give it a boost when you get back into your regimen.

The same is true with martial arts training. We work incredibly hard day in and day out attempting to improve our skills. As an instructor, I make this break mandatory. Every few months we hold a rank testing which can be quite stressful for students. The week following that testing is always fun week. We take off from the normal routine of needing to improve and just go off the page, and not care how well we do and try new things. This break in training is needed to help clear the mind and reset our thinking by taking a step back, or to the side.

Todd Champion (red/white/blue uniform) trying to fluster Jordan, a very serious student who was testing for his black belt, by making him laugh while sparring in a ridiculous uniform. Photo by Dan Bourelle

How many times have you stared at a problem for hours trying to figure it out, whether it be for work or studies, but you just can't figure it out? You finally throw your hands up, give up and go to bed. The next day you wake up to briefly look at the problem and, suddenly, there is the answer. The brain, just like the body, can get in a rut. A break away from the norm can and will do a lot of good.

These breaks don't just happen once a year, once a month or even once a week, but every day. Taking the time to step away from the norm is important to refocus our thoughts, boost energy and challenge the mind/body in new ways. When I say break, I don't mean sitting mindlessly on the couch watching TV, sorry. The body and mind are fully capable of physical and mental stress of action. As long as we have an adequate amount of sleep, we are good to go.

During these breaks it is important to continue to challenge the mind and body. Much like our breaks in martial arts, we don't go easier, we just do things differently. It's analogous to throwing a curve ball at the mind and body. This change can develop our mind and body in new ways which can help boost and energize us while working towards our main goals. In the middle of a tough project? Take a break, pick up a musical instrument and learn how to play it. Or, maybe start learning a new language. Or, write a few paragraphs on the benefits of taking a break!

Take a page from the birds and the squirrels. Take a break from worrying about, seemingly, life or death situations and chase a sibling up a tree or take a swing at a giant stranger...or maybe just read a book.

PART II:

Observations of the Mind

CHAPTER 13

Martial arts tradition and the Easter ham

As a young girl watches her mother prepare a ham for dinner that evening, the girl notices that her mother cuts the ends off of the ham before placing it into the oven. This prompts the girl to ask her mother,

"Why did you cut the ends off of the ham?"

The mother replied, "Well, to be honest, I don't really know, it's a family secret for cooking a great ham I assume. My mother always cut the ends off so I've just done the same."

The mother continued, "Why don't you give your grandmother a call, I'm sure she'll know." So, the young girl called up her grandmother and asked her the same question.

"Grandma, why do you cut the ends off of the ham before you put it into the oven?"

The grandmother paused and thought for a moment and then replied, "I'm not really sure why, that's just the way my mother always did it, so I've always done the same. Why don't you call your great grandmother and ask her? I'd love to know why we've always done that!" The young girl proceeds to call her great grandmother to ask her the same question.

The young girl asked, "Great grandma, why do you cut the ends off the ham before you place it in the oven?"

The great grandmother smiled. "Well that's a simple answer, it's because the pan I used to cook the ham in years ago was too small to fit the entire ham, so I had to cut the ends off to make it fit."

Martial arts are notorious for being steeped in tradition. From the bowing, to the uniforms we wear, to the techniques we use and claim to be useful in self-defense. Much like the story above, we get so focused on doing what we've always done, we forget to stop and ask why we do it. It's when we stop and ask why, that we discover how to better use these techniques, better understand the culture, or even completely remove the technique or drill.

We have to understand the history and the culture behind the martial art being practiced as it will lead to the reasons why we do what we do. For instance, why do we bow? We don't bow anywhere else in Western culture. We shake hands, we salute, but we don't bow. We bow in the martial arts because most all martial arts originated in eastern countries where they greet each other by bowing.

I walked into a Karate school one day to check out the school and meet with the instructor. This school took pride in being known as a "Traditional" Karate school. I've always had respect for these hardnosed martial artists. It was to no surprise that they were punching a makiwara board (hard wall mounted target designed to toughen knuckles) and from what I was told, they use no sparring gear and strike full power as it helps prepare them for a real fight.

What did surprise me was when I spoke with the students; they were not fighters, law enforcement, military or anything of the sorts. They were just your run of the mill civilians, business men and women. All that ran through my mind was,

"Why are average people preparing their bodies for a hand to hand war?" The whole point of learning martial arts as a civilian is to strengthen and protect your body (or another's) from harm, not break it down and make it accustomed to being beaten.

A photo of student, Paulo Almeida, during a photo shoot with photographer Evan Scott.

To each their own. If you enjoy that kind of training, then by all means seek it out. I find; however, many people just blindly follow and do what they are taught without asking why. Tradition is great, as long as it's either needed and/or wanted. When it leads to unnecessary injury and irreversible damage, in my opinion, it needs to be removed.

This obsession with clinging on to tradition is not just limited to martial arts either. It's all over. It's in politics, religion, our workplace and even our schools. While I will not comment on these as they do not pertain directly to martial arts, it's important to understand that the only way to move forward in life is to accept that what we know may be wrong or in many cases, no longer apply to current times. It's imperative that we open our minds and ask "why?" If not, we are doomed to never evolve.

This evolution of martial arts has begun to happen in mid 1990's largely due to mixed martial arts sport fighting, aka, MMA. I've watched many martial arts schools change dramatically since MMA has become mainstream. There is no denying that MMA has helped break people's ties to useless traditions. However, with this break in tradition, I've also found this mindset going too far astray in some cases. Such as suggesting that specific martial arts are better than others or that some techniques aren't useful since you don't see it done on TV. Once again, we must always come back to one word, "Why?" While it's important to trust our instructors and not second guess them, it's crucial to understand what you are learning. It's up to you how to go about doing this. I beg you, please, stop cutting the ends off of your ham and telling people it's a family secret!

While I'm a big proponent of questioning authority and asking why, it's now time for me to contradict myself! Fall in line, do what you're told and don't question my authority!

Ok, let me clarify. There's a time and place for everything, and asking questions is no different. When your boss runs into the room and barks out commands, do you stop him and question his commands? You may find yourself without a boss to question shortly thereafter. Does a soldier stop and ask his commanding officer what the importance is of his orders? I shudder to think of the results of that poorly timed question!

Timing and trust tend to be the biggest factors here. Trust in your superior or instructor that they know best. Admittedly, it's not easy nowadays to trust authority figures and professionals as we are living in an age of being the "Jack of all trades" who dislike their jobs more than the "Ace of your skill" who loves their job. We sometimes blindly trust someone who we assume we should, and it may backfire. Ask questions ahead of time to gain that trust. While it's important to constantly ask "why," it's also important to know when to conform and do what you're told, or what society expects. But you're a rebel and you live by your own rules, right? Even rebels conform. How many people do you see purposefully driving on the left hand side of the road here in the states? No need to stop in the middle of the road and ask "why?" Life just works smoother and more efficiently when we are all on the same page.

Our daily routine is dictated by this order and hierarchy. Parents don't do what their children tell them, okay some do, but they shouldn't. We put our pants on after we put our underwear on, except for Superman, but he has a pass. Hierarchy, order, trust, and timing are what keep things running smoothly and efficiently. I love when students ask me why we do a drill or what the purpose of a technique is, but stopping in the middle of the drill to ask why only reduces your time spent practicing.

Remember to always ask why, just know that sometimes that "why" has to be spoken to just yourself until the right time. Also know that sometimes those questions about technique can many times be answered by practicing. Some of the best answers come from self-discovery.

CHAPTER 14

The weakest creature on the planet

The votes are in and the winner of the weakest creature on the planet is.......THE HUMAN BEING!

When it comes to physical ability, the human being is one of the weakest and most physically pathetic creatures on the planet. Turtles have shells to protect them. Tigers, lions, and bears have sharp teeth and claws. Birds can fly. Even our household pets are more physically adept and agile than we are. To make matters worse, we destroy what little abilities we have with our vices. We inhale cigarettes to hinder our breathing and immune systems. We gorge ourselves with junk food as we sit in front of a TV avoiding physical exertion unless absolutely needed. We poison ourselves with alcohol to further impair our abilities. To each their own. I'm not innocent from these things myself, but it leads you to wonder; how did we get to the top of the food chain?

What is it that we have that no other creature on earth seems to have? For most of us, it's our intellect. I say most of us because I've seen some animals outsmart humans on more than one occasion. No matter how fast, how strong, or how deadly the creature is, humans have always been far superior in handling these creatures by use of our intellect. We set traps, we build weapons, or we are simply smart enough to stay away and not get attacked.

Dan attending the graduation of two of his students, and junior black belts, at an accelerated school that takes students through high school courses in only two years. Griffin Pace (left), Dan (middle), Maisie Boren (right).

What does this have to do with martial arts? Everything. Without the intellect behind our new found physical abilities we are doomed to either injure ourselves or needlessly injure others. We must also understand that our physical bodies have limitations, while our minds, arguably, do not. If we don't train our intelligence alongside our physical abilities, then our physical abilities will never reach their potential. You must ask "why" before fully understanding a technique and its use. We must constantly be aware of what separates us from all other creatures on earth and cater to it.

Good martial artists know how to physically defend themselves in a bad situation. Great martial artists know how to stop a fight before it starts. This is where the mental side conquers all. Most of us fight out of fear. We fear that if we don't, we will get hurt. We fear that if we don't, others will think less of us. We fear that if we don't throw the first punch, the other person will, and we won't get a chance. We fear that we aren't smart enough to fight back with our intelligence when the argument reaches a boiling point, so we fight back with our fists. We fear that if we don't stand up and get in the face of the guy talking to our girl, he'll steal her away. Most folks who initiate fights are insecure, mentally weak, and lack confidence.

Through martial arts training we gain confidence and we learn about ourselves such as our strengths and weaknesses. We prove ourselves to ourselves. When we know and understand our capabilities, we no longer need to prove it outside of the training center. With this knowledge comes the confidence and calmness to not get caught up into arguments that could lead to physical altercations.

Train your strength, train your speed, train your fighting skills, but don't forget to train the most powerful attribute of all, your intelligence.

CHAPTER 15

Le'go my ego

Dan (left) and Master Brent Holland (right) sparring during a fight night where a few area schools got together to spar for a few hours. Photo by Mark Tomes

You stand in the middle of the training center with your brand new brown belt wrapped around your waist. A white belt walks up to you and asks you if they are doing their technique correctly. You correct their technique. With gratitude they say, "Thank you sir! I wish I could be like you someday!" You feel pretty good about yourself.

Several more lower ranks walk up to you, and you help them as well. You're starting to feel important, like you have all of the answers. You're the "go to guy" when the instructor is busy! Then it happens, a lower rank asks you a question that you don't know. What do you do? You can't let them see that you don't have all of the answers. You're status as the "go to guy" is in jeopardy. So, you start rambling, hoping to pull an answer out of thin air. It doesn't have to be the right answer, just has to seem correct. You did it! They bought it! Now back to working on your own techniques.

You have a question, but you can't ask. God forbid the lower ranks see that you don't know everything. Everyone is watching you in awe over how well you flawlessly do your material. Oh no! You've come to that technique that's been kicking your butt lately, you just can't seem to do it correctly. But everyone is watching. You can't look like a fool. You decide to skip it for now. You'll practice it later, you tell yourself. You go back to practicing the techniques you're really good at, you have to keep impressing everyone.

Flash forward a number of years. Not only have you received your black belt, but you've begun teaching. You now have an entire group of students in awe of you and your abilities. "You're the greatest!" they all say. Over the years the hype builds more and more. As it should, they've never seen you make a mistake with any technique. You've always managed to avoid that technique when people are watching.

You answer every one of their questions with confidence, even though many of your answers nowadays are just nonsense you come up with on the spot. The rumors of how you took down five guys in a street fight all by yourself must be true, you told them the story yourself.

And when they ask why you don't teach a certain technique that another instructor teaches, you let them know how ridiculous that technique is and how it would never work, since it's never worked for you, as you have never learned it. And there it is, you're no longer a martial artist, you're a walking egomaniac with a belt around your waist that doesn't even hold up your pants let alone represent who you are.

We all have it. Whether it's from our profession, our hobbies, the sports we play to the sports we cheer for. We all have egos. Some are just more prevalent than others. The martial arts are no different. As a matter of fact, egos tend to run rampant. It seems almost mandatory for an instructor to have an ego. Bow to your instructor. Say "Yes Sir!" or "Yes Ma'am!" Never second guess your instructor. These are really just signs of respect, but they build up that ego just the same if you're not careful.

When the ego grows, the learning stops. We're so afraid of people seeing us make mistakes that we stop learning just to hold on to that ego and that deception of being the best. We think people will stop looking up to us, stop asking us questions, stop being our students, stop respecting us. Maybe. You may have a person or two that only wants perfection so they leave.

Guess what, that was going to happen anyway. No one's perfect and you can't attain something that isn't there. These aren't the people you need around you, learning from you, buying from you, or just standing by you as a friend. I know, I've been there, I've had swollen head syndrome before. It's quite lonely when you place yourself above everyone else and it's a hard drop off of your pedestal WHEN you fall. All we can do is be ourselves and offer our teachings to those who are interested. People may not always follow you, but you tend to have plenty that walk beside you. You'll learn more, create great experiences (not just rumors) and there will always be someone there to pick you up if you fall.

Another photo of Dan (left) and Master Brent Holland (right) sparring during a fight night. Photo by Mark Tomes.

CHAPTER 16

Cows – Nature's killing machines!

While watching the news one day, I saw a story about a shark attack that happened nearby. They mentioned a stat that, while I'm not a violent man, made me want to reach through the TV screen and slap the news reporter across the back of the head. They claimed that you are more likely to be injured by a Chihuahua than a shark. While this is true, it's also incredibly misleading.

It's not that Chihuahuas are more dangerous than sharks, it's that we spend considerably more time around Chihuahuas while we avoid sharks. Sooner or later, you're going to accidentally step on that little rat like dog with a napoleon complex and it will bite you! On average there is only one death per year by shark attack. Why? Because we know how dangerous these animals can be and we avoid them whenever possible.

What kills more people than sharks and Chihuahuas? Cows! Those sneaky little buggers lull you to sleep with their lack of movement and reaction to tipping them over while sleeping, then BAM! They attack! Mind you, cows and bulls are quite large and strong, it doesn't take much to crush you, even by accident. Cows kill, on average, twenty two people a year. What does any of this have to do with martial arts?

Simple, we need to start focusing on training our cow killing techniques. Wait, no, that's not it. Oh yeah, learn to stay away from obviously dangerous places and don't be misled by statistics!

We all know to not walk down a dark alleyway at night all alone, yet we still do. Humans do a lot of stupid things that should be blatantly obvious not to do. Imagine this; you're sitting alone on a bench waiting for a bus. There is little to no traffic and no one else around. A very large, scary, intimidating man sits down right next to you. Mind you he could have stayed standing or sat at the other end of the bench. What do you do?

Far too many people will stay right where they are and say and do nothing. Are people not scared? No, most would be horribly terrified. The problem is that we are even more scared to move as it would seem to be rude to the person who just sat down next to us despite our "spidey senses" going crazy saying this is a bad situation. We are the only creature on earth that ignores its instincts when it comes to safety. We knowingly enter or stay in dangerous situations on a regular basis. This is the cause of many physical attacks.

We've all seen or heard the statistics about violence in America. Statistics suggest one in three women will be a victim of abuse at some point in their lifetime or how every nine seconds a woman is assaulted or beaten. While these are true and horrible, it's not as grim as it seems. We have to understand that these are averages for a large population and wide area. A person from a small town in South Dakota will not have the same level of risk as a person in New York City. Each area is different, some better, some worse.

There is an example I often give when I talk to people about my disgust with most statistics. If there are ten people in a room, five of them are ten years old and five of them are twenty years old, then the average age of the people in that room is fifteen years old, yet there are no fifteen year olds in the room. It's easy to see that averages and statistics don't always represent the truth and can be manipulated quite easily.

How can we sift through all the statistics and discover the truth about how at risk you are of being a victim? You have a couple of options. First, have you ever seen the movie *Bubble Boy*? That's one option. Second, if living your life in a bubble doesn't sound viable, you can simply assess your risks and learn to understand where most crimes and attacks happen so you know how to avoid them or at least be prepared if they are somehow unavoidable.

There is an excellent book written by martial artist and communication skills trainer Nathaniel Cooke called, *How NOT to get HIT: The Art of Fighting Without Fighting*. After extensive research, Cooke identifies personal risk factors and lists them as follows: gender, location, social status, marital status, employment, education level, visits to the bar, and age. All of these categories hold a level of risk depending on the answer. For instance, someone who is a sixty-year-old, retired, married, female, living in a small town and rarely visits the local bars is obviously not very likely to be a victim of a violent crime. On the other hand, a twenty one-year- old single male who is unemployed and frequently visits local bars in a bad area of New York is highly likely to be a victim of a violent crime.

The takeaway here is to learn to trust your instincts. We've spent thousands of years developing them. Be aware of your surroundings and learn about who you are and how your lifestyle can affect whether or not you will become a victim. There is no reason to live in fear if you simply take the time to think logically about who you are and where you are at.

Remember, 85% of statistics are made up on the spot, the other 25% are misquotes.

CHAPTER 17

We can be heroes, but NOT for one day

I was a senior in High School when the Columbine school shootings happened. For those who don't recall the specifics, Columbine High School in Colorado was the setting of a horrible mass shooting by two students in April of 1999. While it wasn't the first school shooting in our history, at the time, it was the largest and was heavily publicized. Twelve students and one teacher were killed, and countless others injured before the two shooters turned the guns on themselves. Their motives? The experts' conclusion was that they wanted attention.

That was the first time in my life that I was made aware of mass shootings of innocent people. Little or no thought was given to a school age student killing fellow students at this point in time for me. It was not something that was ever discussed. My fellow students and I all asked, "Is there anyone in our school that is capable of doing that?" There wasn't a long pause before the same name came up multiple times. We'll call him, "Jonesy."

I was a casual friend with Jonesy and thought he was a good kid, but even I had his name in the back of my brain. Why did we all come up with the same name? It wasn't the music he listened to, it wasn't the movies he watched or which political party he was associated with. None of that crossed our minds. It was the fact that he loved shooting and talking about guns. He was a bit of an outcast. He presented himself in a dark, doom and gloom manner. Jonesy also seemed to be the type that would love to get recognized for getting payback from all who did him wrong. Luckily, I knew him better than that, and knew he would rather crack a joke than shoot at someone.

Yet, when we watched the news over that same week, none of those reasons seemed to be presented for the Columbine killer except as an occasional passing comment. Instead, media and politicians started pointing fingers and blaming all sorts of things as the underlying cause. It was easy to blame musicians (of which the shooters never listened to), guns, video games, movies, and everything else people don't like. Continually watching the same blame game played out with every new mass shooting, while looking past the root cause, is infuriating to me as it fixes nothing.

We see it every time there is a mass shooting or an attempt at one. New day, new shooting, and the same blame game that results in no change. Over the years I've read great books and articles (such as *On Combat,* by Dave Grossman, *The Gift of Fear* by Gavin De Becker and any books from Rory Miller) on the explanations of the shootings and violence. In addition, I have seen similar issues arise in my youth classes, in which we immediately bring them up to the parents and talk to the kids. Even looking back at my days in school I recognized some of the elements at play when issues arose between fellow students.

It seems as though the reasons and answers are there, but no one wants to create the solutions as they aren't as easy as banning music, video games, and guns. The solutions also can't be used as political influence to rally voters around their party or away from the other party. Due to this, the solutions go unapplied. I can't say that what I'll be stating as the causes or solutions are one hundred percent absolute and backed by years of research, but I truly believe in it and many who have done the research have uttered the same explanations. I'm not alone in my thoughts in this chapter, as much of what I've written has been written before, I've just added my flare to it.

There are a couple of things I want to discuss as it relates to mass shootings and how martial arts can be involved in the solution. The first of which is the mental state of an attacker. The second is the mental and physical state of the victim and what they are capable of. Let's start with the mental state of the attacker.

When tragedies like this happen, the first thing on everyone's mind is, "Why did they do it?" There are three major elements that seem to be at play in most, if not all, mass shootings: 1. The person is desensitized to violence; 2. The person is physically trained to kill; and 3. The person has dissociated themselves from the rest of society.

There is an alternate option to these three, which fall in the category of mental disorders. I will not be discussing mental disorders in this chapter as I'm not a medical expert and we simply don't know enough about mental illness, and the connections to killing peers. However, in my eyes, when the three elements listed above are present, it looks like a form of mental illness in itself.

Let's start with element one. There have been many studies showing that children, infants even, are being desensitized to violence in many different ways. A big one being violent scenes on television or even witnessing violence as a child. The delivery system (TV, video games, real life) is irrelevant. At an early age, the child doesn't know if it's real or fake. It becomes normal to them. However, this alone, doesn't create a killer. If it did, I think all of us would be killers. It's just the first step and the first cog in the killing machine.

Element two is the process of being trained to kill. Again, this can happen in many ways. It could be direct training of how to use a weapon of mass killing such as a gun, but in many cases experts have discovered that the mass shooters play a considerable amount of video games that involve shooting and killing. Experts, including elite level snipers, have reviewed the shots from teenagers in some of these mass shootings, and have been baffled by how accurate the shooter is despite never owning a gun until just before the killings. They've concluded that the kids developed shooting accuracy from playing specific styles of video games. This then enabled the teenage shooters to go into autopilot when killing.

Supposedly not every mass shooting was meant to be a mass shooting, the killer only intended to kill one person, but the autopilot took over. It's no surprise that video games can train this process as many professions have made use of video games and simulators to train people's movements, reactions, and skills that can be quickly transferred to real world applications. Again, like the previous element of desensitization, this doesn't mean playing a video game will create killers. It doesn't even have to be a violent video game.

Anyone else grow up with the Nintendo® game, *Duck Hunt*™? I got good at popping those ducks in the head, and the dog on occasion during a bad round. *Duck Hunt* and many others weren't violent video games. For that matter, actual hunting would be the equivalent in this training. Again, that doesn't create a killer. I grew up playing these video games as well as hunting, and shockingly, I've never killed anyone! I hope to keep it that way. This too is just a chunk of the horrifically pieced together puzzle that is the mass shooter.

Last, but definitely not least is element three, being dissociated from society. This is arguably the largest cog in the broken clock brain of a mass shooter. It's also the one that is becoming more and more common and terrifies me. It is not only being ignored on epic levels, but is being fueled by our technology and culture.

Technology has a tendency to pull us away from real life far too easily. It's clear this withdrawal from reality is having a huge negative effect on all of us. The divide and hostility among groups of people is becoming worse due to the lack of true human interaction and misinformation from our trusted media and sources of information. Through these media we see and hear only the extreme points of view and the worst of people, rarely do we see the best and even rarer do we see the normal. With this, our perception gets distorted. Side note, if the media never reported on the Columbine shootings, do you think all the other mass shootings would have happened? Some, yes, most, no. The media essentially implanted the seeds and blueprints to many other copycat shooters.

Within all of us is the potential for violence. We are violent creatures, whether you want to believe it or not. It's how we climbed to the top of the food chain. We were stronger, smarter and more violent than the rest. Don't feed me the lie that you're a lover and not a fighter! If I violently attacked your three-year-old child, would you not come after me with a wrath of violence that even the devil would cringe at? The only thing that keeps our violent nature at bay is our perceived justification for use of violence. We don't attack and hurt those who help us. Generally speaking, anyone we know and come in contact with is typically accepted as someone who can help us unless proven otherwise. Therefore, if our perception of the world is that everyone hates us and wants to hurt us or bring us down, or is so far different from us that we don't see ourselves as the same species, what keeps us from inflicting violence on others? Not a whole lot unfortunately, as it is seen through mass shootings and bombings as well as bullying.

Look at all of those who have committed violent crimes as youth over the past twenty or more years. Note the current year of compiling this book is 2020. A vast majority of these troubled teens were not involved in any group activities and were heavily isolated. They had no outlet in which to be heard or seen or loved by others. Their perception of the world was extremely dark and violent; they themselves felt like the victims and that they were justified in their actions. We all seek acceptance in this world as we are social creatures. It's becoming quite clear that many people accept that recognition is just as meaningful as accomplishment. While accomplishment is achieved through hard work and dedication - generally positive actions - recognition can be achieved easily through violence and with little effort unfortunately.

In an age of "everyone is allowed their fifteen minutes of fame" through social media and reality TV shows, we have everyone spewing forth their inner most thoughts with no filter. That filter tends to be there when directly interacting with others face to face, but it seems to disappear when there is disconnect between faces, such as social media sites or message boards. This unfiltered mess brings out the worst in us.

Then to make matters worse, we are isolated. This isolation removes us from the truth. Isolation plays tricks with the mind and can quickly turn a sane man insane! When were the lowest, most depressing, upsetting moments in your life? Were they when you were surrounded by your friends and family that show love and support for you? Or when you were alone and feeling disconnected from those who love and support you? Maybe after a break up or death of a loved one? We've all had our "hermit" moments where we've hid from the world, but most of us get out of it. Unfortunately, some are stuck there in a downward spiral, and this is where the issues arise.

There's nothing wrong with the technology we have today, it's the amount of time we spend using that technology and watching inaccurate takes from the media that is the problem. Gavin De Becker stated it well in his book, *The Gift of Fear*, when he wrote, "...the bigger issue arises when media consumption replaces the rest of life." Herein lies the problem. We spend more time viewing life and social interaction through media and technology than through actual life.

Now let's discuss the mental state of the victim and how possible it would be for a random person to step up and stop the shooting. In order to understand the mental and physical state of the victim, we must understand the Autonomic Nervous System (ANS). I'll do my best to keep this as simple and as short as possible without going into a biology lesson. The ANS is divided into Parasympathetic (PNS) and Sympathetic (SNS) systems. The PNS is active during non-stressful times where SNS is activated during stressful moments (more commonly known as fight, flight, or freeze.). Most of us have heard, and broadly understand, what the fight, flight, or freeze system is about. When in a highly stressful situation the body discharges a large amount of stress hormones that give us additional strength and enhanced gross motor skills in order to physically "fight" or "flight" when presented with a life threatening situation. For many, though, they "freeze" when this system hits, which is the worst scenario of the three.

Dan teaching at a fundraising seminar. Photo by Mark Tomes.

While it may sound great to have this system pop and have enhanced strength, it is not. It is a last resort for the body in a stressful situation. Enhanced strength and gross motor skills are great, but they come at a cost. First, they only last approximately ten to fifteen seconds. After that, you may be too exhausted to fight efficiently. Secondly, vasoconstriction of blood vessels at the end of the limbs occur, pupils dilate and the digestive process ceases, and in some cases waste is expelled. Third, your complex motor skills (hand/eye coordination, accuracy, etc.) and fine motor skills (grabbing, pulling a trigger, etc.) will be lost or dramatically deteriorated. Last, higher brain function, such as communication and other complex thoughts, also deteriorate.

Let's break this down. When you're faced with an immediate life threatening situation you lose the ability to think properly, lose accuracy and hand/eye coordination, and you're left with the enhanced ability of strength to either punch/kick (with less accuracy) or run away. Does this sound like a good mental and physical state to be in to approach an active killer or really do anything in a stressful situation? Absolutely not!

How do law enforcement, military, and martial artists perform these skills in these situations? They train under stressful situations to teach the body to avoid entering SNS activation through threat recognition, or at least retrain their instinctive skills to react appropriately if it does become activated. Shooting a few rounds at a target at a local shooting range is simply not enough. Nor is casually throwing kicks and strikes in the comfort of your own home learning martial arts from a book, YouTube, or a DVD. This is why we as martial artists spar in class, compete in tournaments, and participate in rank testings in front of large groups. These are all ways to induce stressful situations in which the student needs to perform.

Are guns useless in self-defense? Of course not. What I have written above are facts of what the body goes through during life threatening moments. There are several other factors involved with how an outcome is played, but for the untrained civilian it's all a chance game and the numbers don't go in their favor. It may work out, but probably not.

The simple act of having a gun in some cases can deter a criminal, the same way it can deter you from fighting back when the criminal pulls a gun on you. The intent no longer matters; it's the perception of intent that matters. Many have quoted Admiral Isoruku Yamamoto as stating, "You cannot invade the mainland United States. There would be a rifle behind every blade of grass." While this is a misquote and was never actually said by the Admiral, the statement itself is still quite true.

The perception that every household has a gun and is willing to use it is enough to deter any army from stepping foot on U.S. soil. Unfortunately, none of this applies to mass shooters. Their brain is not functioning the same way a regular mugger with a gun or knife would be. One person approaching them will likely do nothing but lead to another victim. There are suggestions out there that an adult they trust and know yelling out their name and to stop would halt some mass shooters, but unfortunately, the reason they are in this situation is because there weren't a lot of adults around earning their trust to begin with.

We all have those dreams of jumping into action to stop a criminal act in progress, whether it is with your bare hands or with your trusty side kick that you carry in your holster everywhere you go. The fact of the matter is, it's just not going to happen if you're not trained properly, which very few are.

You can't spend your life on the couch or in a cozy office job and suddenly jump up and be a hero. Our heroes are trained, be it through our law enforcement, military or other. It takes a special human being to choose one of these careers and put their life on the line for strangers.

Please, if you decide you want to purchase a firearm for protection, learn everything about that firearm and how to use it in a stressful situation from a professional. Understand that the firearm you are holding is meant for one thing, destroying and killing anything it is pointed at.

I'm not a big fan of pointing out errors in others or in society without providing a solution along with it. While there may be numerous different ways to resolve mass shootings, I believe the biggest point of focus needs to be on the third element, being disassociated with society. It's also the toughest one to fix as it involves everyone making adjustments and not just banning guns or video games or some other quick fix that we ourselves don't have to do. WE need to make adjustments to make this fix, not someone else.

I may be biased, but I believe martial arts can resolve these issues on both the attacker and victim side of things. I'm not suggesting martial arts is the end all be all answer to helping troubled souls, but it's obvious that it helps considerably when taught correctly. I'm looking at you Master John Kreese of the Cobra Kai. It can also train the victims to be not just physically prepared, but more importantly, mentally prepared as martial arts training helps people navigate that SNS (flight, fight, or freeze) process so one can think clearly to escape, call for help or even defend themselves if the other two break down.

Any group activity can be useful, however, when it comes to keeping someone from becoming a killer. Very few, if any, school shooters were involved in group activities, not even music class. These youth turned killers were all isolated and outcasts. Some bullied relentlessly, but not all. It's interesting to note that nearly all mass shooters are boys/men. On what I feel is a related note, the suicide rate is much higher for girls in those same age groups. It makes you wonder if they are connected and the only difference is that most boys lash out and kill as a result, while girls turn inwards and hurt themselves instead of others.

If you find that you or your child is spending far too much time viewing the world through technology and removing themselves from real interactions, I implore you to take steps towards getting them involved in something real. While I may be biased when it comes to martial arts, anything that gets you or your child interacting with others in a positive manner will help dramatically. I find martial arts is one of the few activities that accepts anyone and everyone and consistently boosts physical prowess, awareness, mental sharpness, respect, courtesy, and all around confidence in its participants.

As for the rest of us, we need to do a couple things. One, learn to recognize the behaviors that lead to violence. This too is covered in many martial arts and self-defense classes. Two, recognize verbal and physical cues as well as ongoing behavior. Gavin DeBecker's *The Gift of Fear* is a fantastic book on how to recognize these issues and how to deal with them. I truly believe it should be required reading in school.

On the subject of school, this too is something I've been heavily critical of over the years. Classes on this subject of recognizing threats and how to treat each other as well as how to properly court or talk to potential partners is something that should absolutely be taught in school. Social interaction is a crucial skill that most of us need help with.

I know it would have dramatically changed my school age years. I was very much a wallflower that had no idea how to talk to girls, or anyone for that matter. The last thing I feel we need to do as a society, is to be nicer to each other. There is so much unnecessary hate and anger floating about. Not as much in personal interaction, but through social media and other online sites and programs.

Go watch a random YouTube video on someone showing how to bake a cake, and read the comments. It'll take about three comments in to see a string of obscenity and harsh critiques of the video or people in the video, then followed by replies to that comment filled with more hate and anger. For what? It provides nothing useful to society. With that said, I truly believe we live in a much safer and nicer society than in any time in history, but only in person. Online, it's quite the opposite. So please, go smile and say something nice to someone today!

Now, onto a more light-hearted chapter on guns. Sorry, it'll lighten up soon, I promise!

CHAPTER 18

Boomstick welfare

"Who needs martial arts and self-defense training when I have a gun!"

If you're agreeing with this statement or have ever uttered these words, know that I am doing everything in my power to reach through space and time to slap you across the back of the head as hard as I can. If my hand is unable to reach through, then keep reading so I can at least slap your brain with some facts and a dose of reality.

First and foremost, this is about gun safety as it relates to self-defense, and I have no interest in discussing gun laws or gun control as it is completely irrelevant to this topic. Most people have general knowledge of gun safety, such as keeping it out of reach or hidden from children, understanding how the gun works and competency in shooting the gun with some accuracy. However, there are elements about self-defense and use of a gun for self-defense that seem to elude the general public. If you own a gun, I hope you take this chapter to heart and put to use the suggestions that follow at the end of the chapter.

Let's start with an exercise. I want you to think to yourself, "When would I successfully use a gun to defend myself or others?" Take a moment and think it through. Make sure it's a scenario where using a gun to defend yourself (or others) is the fastest, easiest, most efficient way of dealing with an actual life threatening situation. Be as realistic as possible and recognize any mistakes or problems that may arise from pulling out that gun and shooting another human being. Ask yourself, "Will I accidentally shoot someone I love?" "Will I accidentally shoot an innocent bystander?" "Will I have time to un-holster the gun, aim and shoot accurately?" "Is the death of another human being warranted?" Take your time, this can be a long thought process.

What scenario is going through your head right now? Did you find a perfect scenario? If you're being truthful to yourself and have looked at all the possible issues, such as shooting the wrong person or killing someone that wasn't in the act of attempting to kill you (or someone else), or even having the time and ability to un-holster the gun and accurately shoot, then I think you'll find you came up with very few scenarios, if any at all.

We have to understand the meaning of self-defense. It involves doing just enough to halt a threat towards yourself. That's it. It's not about winning. It's not about getting revenge. It's not about feeling like a hero. This means that if someone runs up to you and steals your wallet and runs off, you can't pull out your gun and kill them. Nor can you even chase them down and "make them regret it." This is murder and assault. You go to jail. Not to mention you just killed another human being. Maybe that person was pure evil and on his way to kill someone, but chances are, he was just looking to get money that he (in his mind) desperately needs. Chances are, many of the scenarios that went through your head involved the use of a gun when it was not only unnecessary but illegal. Hopefully, you recognized that and moved on to another scenario.

We have to understand, for us regular civilians, we are not law enforcement, military, or security guards that are supposed to be trained properly to use a gun, when to use the gun, and how to use the gun. As a civilian, our physical skills, as well as our mental skills of recognizing a true threat, and even properly dealing with the psychological issues that arise from killing another human being, even if they deserve it, are simply not good enough.

With that said, there are times where a gun is not only useful, but your best option, even for someone who is a ninth degree black belt. As I've stated above, self-defense is about the most efficient way of defending yourself, not the most fun way or the way your ego will let you. Violence and threats on your life are nothing to take lightly. If your life depends on it, you have to be ready to do what it takes to survive and keep your family safe. I'm not talking about bar room fights, or arguments between friends/former friends/strangers. Those scenarios are easily avoidable and are not threats on your life.

I want to make something perfectly clear. If someone truly wants to kill you, you will have no choice in the matter. You will simply be killed. If you're lucky, they will make a mistake and you will have a brief moment to defend yourself or escape. Despite what you see in movies, no one jumps out of the bushes and shows you their weapon and says they are going to kill you. They will not give you the option of defending yourself, you will be attacked quickly and efficiently when you least expect it and are least prepared.

If someone shows you their weapon in front of you, it is meant as intimidation and they do not want to use it, they simply want something from you. Mind you, that doesn't mean they won't use that weapon if you don't give them what they want. They just prefer not to as it's in their best interest, as well as yours, not to use it.

A few more things to think about when it comes to using a gun in self-defense. I've mentioned in the previous chapter, and will mention it again in a future chapter, how the body reacts to threats and survival. I don't want to go into great detail here as it's listed in the previous chapter so I will just remind you of some of the effects the body goes through when in survival mode.

When faced with a serious threat the body goes in to the fight, flight, or freeze response. When this happens, cognitive thought ceases. You can't think straight or rationalize, it's simply reaction, even possibly forgetting you have a gun. The blood pulls away from your limbs which leads to the loss of fine and complex motor skills. Reaching for your gun and pulling the trigger fall under fine and complex motor skills. You suffer from tunnel vision - better hope that target isn't moving, or he'll quickly leave your tiny line of sight. These are just some of the negative effects the body goes through instantly when a threat suddenly arises.

You can see how this can cause a nightmare scenario when it comes to recognizing a true threat, un-holstering, aiming, understanding consequences, recognizing if there are innocent people standing by that could get shot by accident, and then pulling the trigger. It's quite simple. If you haven't trained extensively and under duress, which is placing the body into those stressful situations and still performing, then you'll have an extremely difficult uphill battle when it comes to defending yourself with a gun in random and sudden situations.

Are there scenarios in which a gun is the best option? While there are random times and random scenarios, the most common would be home invasions. This is particularly so when all family members are accounted for. When someone has broken into your home, there is generally time to take cover. There is time to get your gun if placed in a proper place. There is time to breathe to calm the nerves and remove negative effects that may have been induced by the SNS kicking in and activating the fight, flight, or freeze reaction. There is also time to think things through and prepare for what needs to be done.

When someone enters your home without your permission, this is someone breaking into the one place that is supposed to be your safe zone, where no one can hurt you or your family and it is not through your actions that this person has become a threat. There is a lot to deal with and think through and prepare for when it comes to a home invasion, far too much for me to explain in this chapter. However, if someone has broken into your home, knows that you're home, and yet remains there, there is simply no "innocent" or "accidental" intent anymore, your life is in danger and you have to prepare to potentially kill someone if you are unable to scare them off.

It was about four in the morning and I am fast asleep. Then, "BOOM!" I wake up in a haze and wonder if what I heard was real or in a dream. "BOOM!" It happens again. "Okay, that's not good" I said to myself as I jumped out of bed and ran into the hallway. My brother, who I was living with at the time, jumped into the hallway at the exact same time. As soon as we both saw each other, we knew it wasn't either of us. "BOOM!" It happens again. It sounded like it came from downstairs. We both rush down.

I run to the back door he goes to the front. I cautiously open the door and search the backyard as I think to myself, "the intruder will most likely leave as soon as he knows someone is home" noting that most thieves just want your stuff and not violence. No one was in the back yard. Then I hear, "I've got a gun, you better leave now," my brother yelled. I run back in and see my brother running up the stairs as I call out to him, "Where is he?!" "He's trying to get in the front door," he replied as he ran upstairs to grab his shotgun. I too run back upstairs to call the police. "BOOM!" He's STILL trying to get in even though he knows we are home!

I suddenly realize we may have to kill someone tonight as that is the only reason I can think of as to why someone would know we are home and still want to break in. I notify the police of the situation as I look out the window to try and gather as many details as I can as my brother stands guard at the front door with shotgun locked and loaded as the intruder continues to try and kick in the door.

I stay on the phone as I head back downstairs as I have all the info I can gather from the window. As I exit my bedroom door, I grab my weapon, my handcrafted Jingum, Korean version of a samurai sword. Then I realize, I don't want to ruin my sword, it cost me more than my first car. Plus, my brother had his shotgun, so my sword wounds would just be insult to injury.

I run back downstairs where my brother is still standing guard at the front door with the shotgun. My brother yelling at the attempted intruder and the man yelling back. I'm still on the phone, mentally and physically ready for something bad to go down. Our dog with fur standing on end, barking at the door ready to pounce! Then in an instance it all changed, with one statement from the attempted intruder.

"This is my house (insert address here) let me in!" My level of worry suddenly dropped. "This moron is on something and thinks he's trying to get into his own house," I thought to myself. With enough reminders that we had a shotgun pointed at the door, he finally decided to walk back to his pick up and drive off. An officer pulled up right after, he had to have passed the truck I described over the phone, but apparently didn't notice with all the other vehicles on the road. It was four in the morning.

Frustratingly, even though we provided his home address that he shouted out during the incident, the police were unable to do anything other than patrol the neighborhood. Rightfully so, it's just our word and no proof. My point of this story is to explain a realistic process that went the best way possible. First, if you've never been suddenly awakened at night to the sound of someone trying to break into your house, it can quickly send you into the sympathetic nervous system (SNS), causing you to not think clearly, forget to call the police, and forget you have a weapon, if you have a weapon.

If you do not, you will feel absolutely naked and vulnerable in the worst way imaginable. Even with my extensive martial arts training, if that intruder got in and had a gun or a knife, the chances of me easily taking care of him (or them) unscathed is not high. If you do stay calm enough to call the police and grab a weapon and prepare yourself, then that's just the beginning.

Now you have to logically figure out how to deal with the situation. Do you display that you are home by screaming and turning on the lights in hopes of scaring the intruder off? Or do you hide the best you can, accepting they will rummage through everything and hope they don't find you? Then if you do confront, or get confronted by the intruder, do you know what to do and what to say?

My situation could have gone very bad if we didn't start yelling at the intruder as he never would have yelled back those magic words notifying us that he thought this was his home. If we didn't do that, he would have eventually made it in, and we would have been forced to shoot and kill him. If all goes wrong and they make it in, are you properly trained and prepared to shoot and kill? Are you ready to deal with the PTSD that will most certainly follow afterward?

Still to this day, years later, even though nothing physical happened in my situation, when I hear a noise in the middle of the night, I still assume it might be someone trying to get in. I have at least one weapon hidden in every room of my house and a mental and physical checklist prepared in case it happens again. Personally, I don't like guns or shooting them. I didn't like hunting when I was younger, but I enjoyed the outdoors and doing things with my father. Yet, I have more than one gun in my home and will use them in a worst case scenario. Thankfully, aside from cleaning them, I've never had to pick up any of my weapons.

For those who own a gun or plan on owning one in the future, I want to finish this chapter with some safety advice and notes that will help give you the best chances at using the gun correctly and not firing the weapon at the wrong person or by accident. Please understand, this information is just a small amount needed to be a responsible gun owner. These are just the things that generally get little or no attention and aren't always thought about with gun owners I've spoken to over the years.

Keep any and all guns in a lockbox that only you or another competent adult knows the combination to. I know, you want to keep a loaded gun under your pillow for when you are suddenly woken up by a killer and have only just enough time to grab the gun and shoot to kill. Stop watching movies, seriously, and if you don't, know that everything about them are fake. They are not instructional videos. Keeping your loaded gun under your pillow, or anywhere close by to where you can shoot without thought is a disaster waiting to happen. If someone breaks into your home, you will most likely hear them before they get anywhere near you. If not, you will already be dead before you wake up if that is their intent, so in either situation, that gun under your pillow isn't going to help.

If the gun is in a lock box with a combination, it doesn't take long to open, but long enough to give you time to breathe and assess the situation rationally, hopefully. It keeps the gun out of the hands of a child as well as anyone who may break in. Just make sure your child is not anywhere nearby when you use the combination. You'd be amazed how much information kids retain when you think they aren't paying attention!

Do understand though, like anything else, you have to practice entering the combination and opening the box. It has to be instinctive. As mentioned above, your cognitive thought could be out the window and you'll struggle to enter the combination. Constant practice can dramatically help this and make it instinctive so there is little to no issue. Side note, calling 9-1-1 should also be practiced to instinctive motion for the same reasons. There are many cases of people not only forgetting the number, but unable to dial the numbers due to the lack of fine motor skills while in the fight, flight, or freeze response.

Get proper training. This does not mean going to the firing range on a regular basis. You have to train in a stressful environment to be able to properly use a gun in a stressful situation. Many training systems make use of airsoft guns that don't fire real bullets but have a realistic firing experience backed by realistic scenarios. Again, we're talking about law enforcement/military/security training, which is not easily available to civilians.

Therefore, join a good martial arts school. While we may not use guns on a regular basis, though I feel it should be a part of any martial arts curriculum, we constantly train in stressful scenarios and teach how to calm yourself and not let fear take over which is what leads to the negative effects by entering fight, flight, or freeze. Do understand though, the only perfect training tool for these scenarios is to actually have experienced these life-threatening scenarios. It doesn't matter how well prepared you are, you will make mistakes if you've never actually been in a real fight or life-threatening situation.

Understand the physical and psychological ramifications of killing another human being. If you shoot and kill someone that was not a threat to your life, or was an innocent bystander, you may spend the rest of your life in jail. Know that the act of killing another human being is against human nature. The psychological damage that comes afterwards can be debilitating. There is a reason why PTSD (post-traumatic stress disorder) runs rampant through military and law enforcement. At least they have been prepared for it these days and have a system set up to minimize it, such as debriefings, available counseling, and coworkers that have gone through the same thing to help them through it. The average civilian does not have most of these tools, and what they do have available, they may not know how to make use of.

Finally, understand what you think will happen when you shoot someone is probably not realistic. If you successfully shoot someone in self-defense, they will not go flying back ten feet and die instantly. Again, you need to stop watching and believing movies. A gun shot, through the heart or through the head, will not necessarily kill or even stop someone instantly. That person may continue attacking you for numerous seconds if not minutes before dying. This is especially true if the person doesn't know they've been shot. This is useful information on two accounts. One, you must assume that you cannot instantly kill someone just because you shot them, it has to be a dead on shot and even then, it's not likely to be instant. Two, if you yourself are shot, don't allow yourself to believe you are going to die. You must continue to fight, what have you got to lose? There are numerous accounts of people being shot through the heart and head that have gone on to both fight off a threat and even survive.

We seem to live in a gun crazy society, and worse yet, a paranoid and misinformed society. This is a deadly combination. From movies that glamorize violence and over dramatized killing, to media and politicians that either tout guns as our savior from violence or blame guns as if the gun had a consciousness of its own. We live in a world full of misinformation about guns, violence, and self-defense that is nothing short of appalling. Understand that our greatest weapon is knowledge. Knowledge of yourself, others, your weapons, violence, self-defense, and human nature in general. If you refuse this knowledge, I ask that you please stay away from me, my friends and family as far as possible, thank you. Oh, and if you suggest that you don't need self-defense training because you have a gun around, be prepared for a vicious slap to the back of the head followed by long drawn out ramblings of the information in this chapter.

CHAPTER 19

Special is the new normal

Andrew Arabian is focused and patiently waiting for a class photo while chaos ensues around him. Photo by Sata Bun

I get a call from a parent inquiring about getting her child into martial arts classes.

"Excellent! How old is your child so I know which class to suggest?"

"He's just a few months away from turning four."

"Unfortunately, I don't suggest training that young. I would suggest between six and eight-years-old."

"Oh, don't worry, my child is way ahead of other children his age and is very well behaved for his age and super smart!"

"Well, I guess I can let him try a class, but know that it's highly unlikely it'll work out."

"Awesome! You won't regret it, he's going to be your best student!"

The mother brings her child in for a trial class. Class does not go well. The child doesn't understand what we are doing and just wants to jump on bags and act like a power ranger and listens to nothing I am explaining or demonstrating. I spend the entire class trying to keep him on task and attempting to explain what I want him to do. He cries to his mom that he's bored and wants to go home. His mom obliges and states, "I guess he didn't like martial arts as well as I thought he would," as she leaves, never to return, and most likely never to even try another class when he's of an appropriate age.

This wasn't any specific situation, but every situation when a parent is convinced that their child is special and ahead of the curve. Sadly, this is an all too common occurrence. Parents have a tough time accepting that their child is normal, and make excuses as to why the class didn't work out. It's either my fault, or the child was not into martial arts as much as they thought. This leads me to the focal point of this chapter.

You are not special. Okay, maybe I should elaborate on this as it seems a bit cruel to say it so directly. What I mean is, if we are all special, then none of us are special. I know, I know, we're all special in our own way. I get that and I believe that too, but generally speaking, we are all quite average. I'm not trying to deflate anyone's self-esteem or hurt anyone's feelings but if we all go through life thinking that we are better than everyone else, we're in for a huge disappointment.

It's not our children's fault for believing they are better than everyone else, nor is it really the parents fault as it is their job to make their children feel special. Society on the other hand has been trying a little too hard lately to make everyone feel like we are all on the same playing field in every category, and that simply is not a responsible thing to do. Instead of giving out first, second and third place trophies at competitions, we now give out the same medal or trophy to all the competitors.

More and more schools nowadays are allowing children to pass even with failing grades, no matter how bad they do or how little effort they put into their studies. We seem to be teaching our students that it's okay not to work hard as we will all win in the end. This may boost some kid's confidence at early ages but it will only crush them as they enter the real world where they will be completely unprepared for hard work or failure. It's building a false confidence, which can be very dangerous.

We must understand, that even though we may be born equal, we weren't all created the same. We can't all be professional athletes. We can't all be doctors or astronauts. It's not that it's impossible, it's just implausible. Anything is possible, but we must know our limitations so that we can understand our potential and set realistic goals. From that starting point we can then shoot for the stars!

To tell a five foot two inch teenager that he can be a pro basketball star is most likely to end in heart break and lost time. On a similar note, have you ever seen a professional athlete in person? Or better yet, have you played alongside of one? I had the misfortune of facing two pitchers when playing high school baseball that were both expected to go straight to the major leagues from high school. Both could throw ninety miles an hour consistently and accurately for six innings straight. These were men playing against children. It wasn't fair. I don't care how good you think you are, very few possess the physical abilities these people have. Yet they too, don't possess the abilities that you have. That is what makes us different, yet equal all at the same time.

As it pertains to martial arts, I'm seeing a larger number of schools allowing their students, young and old, to gain rank just because they've paid their dues for the month or for their rank testing. While every school has its own set of requirements, I find it to be a bad idea to allow students to believe they are deadly weapons based on the fact that they have a black belt around their waist. This false sense of security and confidence could put their life in danger if they happen to find themselves in a situation in which they have to physically defend themselves.

On the rise are parents thinking their child is more advanced than other children and that they should be given special treatment, or allowed into a program that they aren't old enough for. They are suggesting their child is a prodigy. While I love the fact that they want to get their children into martial arts at a young age, the fact of the matter is I have only seen maybe one or two children in the twenty five plus years I've been involved with martial arts that I would consider prodigies. I've always given the parent the benefit of the doubt. The results are usually the same; a deflated child who becomes turned off by martial arts and never wants to return due to the fact they were unable to pick it up as fast as expected, or were unable to understand what was being taught.

Again, I'm not trying to mentally beat down you or your child, quite the opposite in fact. The issue at its core, in my judgment, is due to the overwhelming sense that we need to lump everyone together into the same imaginary mold. By telling everyone they are special in the same ways as everyone else, we are eliminating the fact that everyone is special in their own ways, therefore everyone is considered the same and special is no longer special. We need to stop attempting to fix problems by lumping everyone together just to make it easy to fix. We end up implying that one person is special in a category they are not special in and implying that another person is not special in a category that they are special in. There is no one solution to fix all the problems. Sorry, I know that may be the easy way, but it's just not working. We and our children are unique and special in our own ways, and the rules, laws, and guidelines must be adjusted on the go. There is simply no other way. One size does not fit all.

CHAPTER 20

Objects in the rearview mirror may NOT be as close as they appear

(A guide to accomplishing your New Year's resolutions)

Every January I get an increase in phone calls and email for both martial arts classes and personal training. Only about ten percent of those inquiries, however, turn into regular students or clients. Why? There seems to be a few common issues that lead to the eventual failure of attaining one's New Year's resolutions.

The first issue is setting unrealistic goals. It's great to have that large goal, but you need to set smaller goals to reach that larger one. Martial arts teaches this goal setting perfectly. Not only are there multiple color belt ranks to attain before you reach black belt, but there are ranks within those color belt ranks. Students are attempting to reach a goal every time they are in class. Remember to be realistic with what you want to accomplish. You don't have to do everything in one year.

The second issue, and probably the most important, is failing to adjust one's lifestyle to accommodate the goal. For instance, many people want to get into better shape, however, they only add in occasional gym workouts when it fits into their current schedule and forget the importance of nutrition. This simply doesn't work.

One must completely adjust his/her lifestyle to support regular exercise and healthy eating to accomplish that goal.

Have you decided to take up martial arts training? How many nights are you setting aside to train? I have many students that can only afford or only have time for one night a week to come into an organized class. There's nothing wrong with that, but if that's the only night you even think about class, let alone train, you're doomed to stay at the beginner ranks. Take time to set up a schedule to cater to your new training. Also make sure and remove bad habits that eat up your time and replace them with good habits that make use of your time wisely. Log off of Facebook® for an hour or two, and put down that video game controller and get something done. We all need time for enjoyment and relaxation, but we don't need eight hours a day of it.

The third issue is perceived timing. You know what I'm talking about here. We've all uttered the words, "This week isn't a good week, I'll start next week." Procrastinator!!! I know, I know, but the economy isn't very good right now, there's a deadline at work that you have to concentrate on first, or maybe it's raining outside, nothing gets done on rainy days, right?

I'll let you in on a secret. I'll give you the equation to figure out when the best time is to start. Come closer, a little closer, I don't want anyone else to see this. The equation is a + c − b = now you fool, now! There is no perfect time, so stop looking for it. In the words of the great philosopher Nike®, "Just do it." I'm going to be brutally honest here. Your quality of life will not improve without massive amounts of effort to improve it. Sorry. Wishing and dreaming is pointless without the action to make it a reality. If you feel these "perceived timing" issues are more important than improving the quality of your life, then so be it. I'll make sure and wave at you when I see you in my rearview mirror.

So what's it going to be? What do you want to improve in your life? Are you willing to put it in writing? You're much more likely to attain your goals when you write them down or announce them to friends. Write out how you will go about attaining your goals. Then begin your journey.

When I was about twelve-years-old, my father surprised me at Christmas with an electric guitar that I asked for but never expected to receive. I had tried violin and tuba in grade school, both I hated and didn't want in the first place. I chose the violin when I first wanted to play guitar because my school didn't offer guitar and the one base (the large kind) was already taken. Violin was the only thing left. I had no interest in it and therefore never learned anything more than an ear piercing version of "Mary had a little lamb."

Then in fifth grade we were given more options, but still no guitar. So I chose the drums. After attempting a short drum roll on the side of the table, the band instructor said I'd be a great tuba player. I hated it. Especially the part where I had to clean out the spit drain from the last student who used the tuba, who I'd spotted many times eating his own boogers. It was revolting. So, I quit that too.

The next year when my father asked what I wanted for Christmas, it was a guitar, what I wanted all along. He mentioned only being able to afford an acoustic one, but I complained that it would be easier to play an electric one as the "electric" part does all the hard work. That's a twelve-year-old's logic at its finest. When I actually opened up that present and saw an electric guitar instead of an acoustic one, I was thrilled. I was about to be the next Jimmy Hendrix!

Dan at the age of 12 posing with his electric guitar.

The following week we went to sign up for guitar lessons at the music store where my father had purchased the guitar. They said they were swamped, but would give us a call later in the week to schedule a time for the first lesson. A few weeks went by and they never called. So we went back, and again, they said how swamped they were but would call later in the week to schedule a lesson for sure this time.

A few months later, we realized they still hadn't called. I tried a few times to play it on my own, but to no avail. So we went back yet again. This time, the store was shut down. No lessons coming from that place. We searched and tried some private lessons, but they were either too expensive or the teacher didn't show up.

At a video store a few years later I found a, How to Play Guitar VHS® in the discount bin for about five dollars. For those that don't know, a VHS is the 80's version of a DVD but you must be kind and rewind before returning it to the store. So I quickly snatched it up and ran home, dusted off my guitar, popped in the VHS and was set to be the next David Gilmour. First up, how to tune your guitar. I knew I was missing a step. I followed the directions on screen the best I could and then went on to learning the first chord. Got my fingers in the perfect position, just like the video. A beautiful sound came flooding out - from the video, not me. My chord sounded like a dying cat choking on a dying mouse. What did I do wrong? I tried numerous times, to no avail. I went back and tried to tune the guitar again as told, thinking maybe I made a mistake. Still no luck. I gave up in frustration and never finished watching the video.

Fast forward about twenty years. Its New Year's 2012. I'm talking to George, a parent of one of my students, about how he went to school for music as well as discussing his playing of the guitar. I had an idea. "Any chance you'd be up for a trade? I'll teach you martial arts, you teach me how to play my guitar?" I asked. "Absolutely," George smiled. It was on!

That became my new year's resolution. George and I scheduled a time slot once a week before class for him to teach me guitar, and I decided to set aside thirty minutes a day to practice what he taught me. The first thing I learned? That I'm tone deaf. That's why I couldn't properly tune my guitar from that VHS all those years ago to make that chord sing. Luckily, he taught me how to tune my guitar with a phone app. Twenty years after receiving one of the best gifts I've ever been given, I was now playing my favorite songs on my guitar. I had finally become the next Stevie Ray Vaughan's physically challenged brother. I accomplished a goal because I took the effort to actually schedule time to practice.

The following year I decided to learn Spanish to better communicate with a family I was teaching at the time. I set aside thirty minutes a day to use my Rosetta Stone® – Spanish addition. For about three months I studied and attempted to understand what that family was saying in Spanish. I struggled. I thought I was getting better at Spanish, but I couldn't seem to understand much of anything being said.

Eventually, after months of learning, I got frustrated with still not being able to understand what they were saying, so I finally asked the mother, Carolina. "I've been trying to learn Spanish for months now to better understand and communicate with you and your family, but it's not working. What am I missing here?" I asked. "Why are you learning Spanish? We speak Portuguese," Carolina responded. This is the day I learned that Brazilians speak Portuguese and not Spanish.

I had violated my first rule I mentioned at the onset of this chapter, "setting unrealistic goals." Attempting to understand Portuguese by learning Spanish is an unrealistic goal. The point of this story is to explain that you need to fully understand and plan out your goals, whether it be resolutions or just decisions to make a change, planning is important. Leave those past failures and mistakes in the rearview mirror of life and don't let them deter you from new goals. Look back on them to learn from them, then focus on what's in front of you and move forward.

CHAPTER 21

Signaling to turn left, while turning right, but should have gone straight

Youth student, Jose Hernandez, missing his target and mistakenly kicking his holder, Jakob Strickland. Photo by Joe Berry

Your instincts can lead you to a good decision, warn you of impending doom, find love, and can even be the death of you. Yes, that instinct you rely on can flat out lie to you. Generally speaking, your instincts come from unconscious recollection of past memories and/or your instincts which developed thousands of years ago through evolution. Or for the creationists out there, "God's nudge."

Our logic and rational thinking come from more conscious thought, past experiences, and overall knowledge we have gathered throughout life. This comes from a "higher reasoning" brain function that evolved more recently on the evolutionary scale. Have I lost you yet? Stick with me, it does relate to martial arts.

Essentially, much of your instincts were developed thousands of years ago for survival purposes. Some of these are still relevant today, others are not. What we need to understand is that our "gut instincts" are simply warning signals, nothing more. It takes our logical, rational thought to judge whether or not these signals are to be taken seriously or not.

Remember the flight, fight or freeze response I spoke of in Chapter 17, We can be heroes, but NOT for one day? When the brain makes the assumption of a threat towards the body, it reacts by going into survival mode. It releases hormones that boost strength temporarily, dilates pupils, and pulls blood away from appendages, including the brain affecting rational thought. These things are meant to help you survive an attack, not fight off an attack with efficiency. The key word in that previous statement is "assumption." The brain made an assumption based on previous experience and survival instincts. If your fire alarm goes off, do you immediately call the fire department, grab the fire extinguisher, break down closed doors and start spraying everywhere going into hero mode? Of course not, in most cases you just cuss under your breath that you have to now get up and figure out what just set it off. Did the food you're cooking produce smoke? Did Uncle Larry light up a cigar? Or are the batteries just dying and the alarm went off to let you know? This is where our logic and rational thought come in. We investigate and determine our best course of action.

Fear, hunger, thirst, goose bumps, love, pain, the list goes on. These are all just warning signals that were developed through evolution to help keep us alive. They are also signs that could be lying to us. Through experience, training, and logical thinking, we can control and/or prevent these signals from affecting us in a negative way. Eat a lot of sweets? Your body will begin to send signals to eat more sweets, even if you are full. Drink a lot of alcohol? Your body will send signals to drink, even if you are not thirsty.

I could go into depth on each one of the above listed signals but I want to stick to the martial arts aspect. Let's go back to the body's reaction to a perceived attack. Without training, the body has one of three options; run from the attacker, violently fight it off by any means necessary, or freeze and lock up. Using extreme violence is fine if your life is in danger, but most of the time it is not. Most attacks are from people you know or drunks at the bar. Violent reactions and attempts on a person's life are not self-defense. They are illegal. You may have defended yourself against a drunken bar fly, but you just landed yourself in jail for life.

It's only through proper martial arts training that folks can defend themselves correctly and within the limits of the law. Or better yet, recognize that there is no threat even when your body may go into the fight, flight, or freeze mode. Many high ranking martial artists will tell you, the ultimate attainment of physical self-defense is not only protecting yourself, but your opponent as well.

We re-wire our instincts through training to defend ourselves properly when needed. We also intelligently think through situations and scenarios ahead of time during training knowing that rational thought may not be available during the fight, flight, or freeze reaction. Many times the "assumed" threat, isn't even a threat. That creepy guy walking up to you reaching in his pocket? Your instinct may scream "attack!" but maybe he's just asking for directions and pulling out a map or his phone? Wouldn't you feel stupid pummeling the poor guy? I'm guessing he and the police won't see things your way! Understand, in that situation, there are steps one should take to make absolutely sure there is no threat as there just might be. This is something covered in martial arts/self-defense classes.

Did you jump into a car and fly down a congested street when you were sixteen before you learned how to drive and before you got your license? No worries, you played plenty of Pole Position™ at the arcade! (Did I just date myself on that reference?) Of course not, that would be stupid. So why do we think we can suddenly defend ourselves properly without any training? You can't.

Please, understand that instincts are just warning signs, nothing more. Have I said that enough times yet? We have to take the time to understand what these signals are and how to react to them. If not, those little love butterflies in your stomach could lead you right into the arms of a killer! There was an interesting study done by Cornell University that relates to this chapter in a couple ways.

This study sought to determine if we can spot a criminal just by a headshot. The study concluded that we can, but we struggle to differentiate between violent and non-violent criminals. Our instincts are there. They can keep us out of trouble if we just understand how to actively listen to our instincts. We clearly struggle with this, though, as we haven't depended on these instincts in a very long time. This brings me to the second way this study relates to this chapter. The researchers also discovered that women were less likely to recognize a rapist than men, based on just their headshot. The study speculates that rapists purposefully make themselves seem non-threatening to accomplish gaining access to their victims.

My point is this – while our gut instinct is still very much alive in us and trying to send us signals to survive, the ability to decipher those signals has deteriorated. We must take the time now to train for self-defense. Don't just trust an evolutionary process that occurred thousands of years ago. There have been more than a few changes in lifestyle in the past 10,000 years.

CHAPTER 22

Soft as a rock, hard as a pillow

*Dan (black uniform), mid-throw of his
training partner during a Hapkido seminar*

Most have heard of and have a general understanding of yin and yang. Most understand that they are opposites, one is hard the other soft, one black, the other white. However, most don't fully understand that they are one in the same as one cannot survive without the other. Another misconception is how it works in the martial arts.

I would like to start by explaining, especially for my students and those who train in the Korean arts, the Yin/Yang symbol on the Korean flag is known as Taegeuk and is represented as a red and blue symbol. The meaning and philosophy are much the same though.

While yin and yang are opposites, one hard, one soft, or one positive, one negative, the fact is, they are always present at the same time. There is no left without a right, there is no fast without slow, there is no wet without dry. Many folks try and separate these opposites in the martial arts. Some arts are known as "Hard" or "Yang" style arts, while other arts are known as "Soft" or "Yin" style arts. While it's true that some arts focus on one attribute over the other, the fact is, all styles have elements of hard and soft.

Take Taekwondo or Karate for instance, widely known and advertised as a "hard" style martial arts since they lean towards force verses force. Hard strikes, hard kicks, hard blocks. However, listen to any coach or instructor while you're sparring and there's a good chance you'll hear him/her tell their student to "relax!" Staying relaxed will allow greater speed, conserve energy, control heart rate and allow a student to maintain balance if struck by a hard strike. Even while kicking and striking there are elements of softness going on. Sliding out to the side of an oncoming attack and flowing through combinations rather than forcing out of sync techniques are elements of yin (soft) within yang (hard).

How about those "soft" style arts such as Tai Chi or Aikido known for their flowing, gentle movements? Are there elements of hardness in these? Absolutely. While all of the techniques may be soft, there is still need for force, albeit minimal. Mind you that it also takes a "hard" attack to create a "soft" defense. Without that hard attack, there will be no soft defense.

Even through physical resistance (hard), softness can be beneficial at the exact same time. Let's do a demonstration.

This is a neat trick you can do with a friend. This is a demonstration of ki power used in Aikido known as the "unbendable arm." I don't mean to offend those who believe in this ki power, I just want to point out that in this scenario, this demonstration can be explained through biomechanics and kinesiology, the study of the mechanics of body movements.

Have your friend hold their arm straight out in front of them. Step up near them so that their outstretched arm is on your shoulder. Place both of your arms onto the bicep or inner elbow, ready to pull down in an attempt to bend their elbow. Tell them to resist your attempts to bend their elbow, moving their hand near their shoulder. You can attempt to bend their arm any way you like, this is just the easiest. Depending on the strength and height difference between you and your friend, you should be able to bend their arm without too much trouble.

Now tell your friend to focus pointing their arm at a distant location and not to lose focus on pointing their arm straight. Follow the same directions as above and attempt to bend their elbow. What did you notice? If done properly, you will find that you are suddenly unable to bend your friend's arm, or at least it became much more difficult. Why is this? It's because in the first attempt, the friend contracted all the muscles in their arm at once in an attempt to resist the bending. This includes contracting the biceps, the muscles that actually cause the arm to bend. This means they were actually helping you bend their arm.

In the second attempt, by focusing on pointing their arm in the distance, the body switches gears and fires off a different combination of muscle groups to resist and relaxes all of the others, namely the bicep. Without the biceps countering the effects of the triceps (the back of the arm), the arm suddenly becomes many times stronger. As you can see, the arm became "unbendable" and stronger by contracting the triceps (hard) and relaxing the biceps (soft). Once again, opposites are working together in unison. Also note how focusing the mind on a different task can make a dramatic difference. The brain and body are mind-blowingly amazing if we just take the time to learn how to make use of them.

We use this same technique while grappling. We rest muscles groups that aren't necessary at the moment while contracting other muscles groups to accomplish the desired action in order to conserve energy. Most novice grapplers fail miserably at this, contracting every muscle in their body at once. I've watched high level, well-conditioned athletes become physically drained within just a minute or two of a grappling session, while lesser conditioned, supposed "non-athletes" who have been training in grappling for an extended period of time can last ten, fifteen, even thirty minutes!

Yin and yang are laws of nature that are prevalent in every aspect of our lives, not just in the martial arts or eastern cultures. Just remember, there is no success without failure, there is no appreciation for heaven without experiencing hell and for every down there is an up. We just have to recognize these opposites when they show themselves.

CHAPTER 23

Mind your "you's" and "me's"

I need you to get me into better shape.

I need you to teach my child discipline.

You're going to get me to black belt, right?

Can you help me get into better shape?

Can you help me teach my child discipline?

What do I have to do to earn my black belt?

While all of these statements and questions may look similar and even lead down the same paths, only three of these lines will lead to success. You and You're versus Me and My. I can't create success for you, but I can provide the opportunity for "you" to create success.

Maybe its intuition, or my amazing powers of observation, or just experience of seeing the same end result over and over, year in and year out, I don't know. I can usually figure out if a new client or student will be successful within just a few minutes of talking to them. I think most teachers, instructors, coaches and trainers recognize the same thing. Simple words like "you" or "me" are indicators of your mindset, outlook, and chance of success in what I'm about to teach you. While I don't lower my efforts with someone who has the "you" mindset, I tend to go above and beyond for those who are self-driven.

I've had many parents bring in their children looking for me, alone, to "fix" them or teach them discipline. While I'm glad they brought their child to me and am always glad to help, the fact of the matter is, I can't change your child's attitude or lack of discipline on my own. A couple of forty five minute classes a week is not enough time to spend with a child to do much of anything other than teach them some techniques. Parents need to be heavily involved to make the needed adjustments.

This same thing is true for those looking to improve themselves. The effort, hard work, and desire have to come from the student or client themselves. It's like the old saying goes, "You can lead a horse to water, but you can't make him drink." It doesn't matter what I teach or how I teach it. If that teaching isn't absorbed, nurtured, and practiced, then it's all for nothing.

Not everyone is given the same opportunities in life, and many have to work harder than others to accomplish their goals, but no one has been banned from achieving success. All are free to attain it, but it has to come from them, not from others. It's easy to depend on others for our success, that way we can blame others when it's not attained. If we spend our lives depending on someone else to create our success or for the pieces to fall perfectly into place before we begin working for our success, then we'll never be successful. Our happiness and success are in our own hands, not others. Change your "you's" to "me's" and alter your mindset to clear way for self-attained success!

CHAPTER 24

I see your mystical and raise you my reality!

Since the beginning of time mankind has always searched, created and believed in something beyond our perceived reality. Examples include mythical beasts, gods, mind altering drugs, magic, and anything that isn't within our current grasp of understanding or removes us from reality. We are not a content creature, and reality never seems good enough. And the martial arts have proven no different. Why do we search for the greener grass of magic when reality is just as mysterious and amazing and sitting within our own back yard?

From super human strength to being indestructible, every martial artist has heard the stories of old time instructors using ki/chi power to demonstrate feats of strength and mysticism. They're great stories, but are they real? I honestly don't know. I will say, I choose not to believe in them until proven otherwise, however. I have no interest in wasting my energy trying to attain something that might be there, when I can place all of my energy into something that is there.

Upon watching demonstrations or hearing old stories of past instructors, don't be quick to dive into the practice of the mystical arts and spending eight hours a day meditating, or going on an all dirt diet, or spending a month naked on a snowy mountain to supposedly attain such incredible skills. First, one must ask oneself a few questions.

Where did it start? It's tough to say where the origins of ki energy and the techniques used came from. However, it is known that both ninja clans and samurai not only welcomed the thought of being other worldly in their abilities, but actually went to great lengths to produce this mystical image of themselves to help build fear in their enemies on the battle field. What better way to mentally destroy your opponent than to make them believe you have god like powers not from this earth?

Dan holding a jingum during a photo shoot with photographer Evan Scott

I believe this is where much of the mysticism came from, but not all. If you knew nothing of the martial arts and saw me place a man larger than me to his knees, crying in pain, just by touching him with my finger, you would think it's magic, would you not? Especially if you were that person being dropped to your knees. However, it's not magic, it's science and knowledge of the human body that can create that scenario.

Yet, if I never told you, you would go on believing it was magic. And what if I showed you how to do it, but never explained why it worked? And what if you turned around and taught it to someone else, but since you didn't know the science behind it, you taught it as magic, or ki power? You would then have mystical techniques that work, but aren't understood.

I believe this is a very likely scenario in the martial arts world. Many instructors forego explaining how techniques work to their students, they just need to make sure their student knows how to do it, asking why doesn't seem important to some when it works. Whether or not ancient martial arts instructors once knew how these techniques worked scientifically, or if they just experimented and saw the end result and taught it, is not known.

Science, however, is learning more and more about eastern medicine and eastern martial arts techniques and beginning to un-mystify them with scientific explanation. One by one, the mysticism is turning into reality by science. Those endless hours of meditation to cultivate ones ki energy to perform amazing demonstrations, just might be knocked down to a ten minute biomechanics lesson.

What's the point? When would this be useful? Why should I dedicate decades of my life practicing hours on end to learn these techniques? The unbendable arm, being "glued" to the ground and unable to be lifted, producing heat from the hands, standing one's ground when being pushed by multiple people, taking a kick to the family jewels, all of these are examples of ki power being used to demonstrate its power. They are fun to watch, but what use are they beyond demonstration? Not to mention, the majority of those demonstrations I just mentioned, I could teach you how to do in one short class.

Never having your arm broken, never being thrown off balance, these are useful things in a fight or even in daily life, but why have I never seen them used in a realistic situation? Why are there always rules to how one can attempt to lift, bend, or kick? Why does the person performing these demonstrations have to prepare themselves and do breathing exercises before the demonstration can be done? Does this not render it useless in a real situation? Note that I have made use of the science behind these techniques, but never the exact technique.

I have so many questions that have never been answered. If the answer is that there is no preparation needed to perform these demonstrations and they can be used in a real scenario, then does that mean that these people never get illnesses, bumps, bruises, cuts or even fall off balance throughout their entire life? Why do I not believe this?

I love the stories, the demonstrations and am open to being proven wrong, but as it stands, all of these demonstrations can be explained through reality, kinesiology, anatomy, biomechanics, or science in general. It may not be the answer, but I have to bow to science when it does provide answers.

Reality more amazing than mystic? What's more interesting and amazing? A mystical energy that flows through your body and can be manipulated to create unique demonstrations, or the fact that the human body has evolved in ridiculously amazing ways that we have only begun to tap into and understand? For me, the human body is utterly amazing and incredible. The more I learn about it, the more I'm blown away by it and how seemingly impossible it is to be as perfect as we are in our functionality. We're not just muscle and bones that move around, we're an incredibly fragile, yet resilient system of billions of things working together to make us who we are and keep us alive.

For instance, when the body is faced with a life threatening situation, it jumps into action. Your senses are heightened, you gain clearer vision, hear clearer, are more focused, and stronger. This assumes you've trained this system appropriately and haven't let fear take over and leave you with tunnel vision, unable to physically move and unable to mentally process what needs to be done. The body can actually shut off its hearing if it's unnecessary or will conflict with actions to save its life. A loud bang can go off near your ear and you won't even hear it, nor will there be any ringing or damage in the ear afterward.

The body, if trained properly, can even go on autopilot and do physical actions without thought or consciousness in times of stress. When in a heightened sense of awareness, the eyes can actually illuminate in the darkness in order to see clearer, almost as if a light was switched on. These bodily functions seem like magic, but are based in reality. The human body is incredible. The reality of what the body can do goes far beyond the mysticism that's flooded through the martial arts. In my opinion, reality is far more incredible than the mystical.

This discussion comes up in my classes from time to time and I always give the following explanation. If I drop a tennis ball from head level onto a wooden floor, I don't assume it's magic or God's will or that the ball enjoys the floor, I know it's gravity. I know it's just science and I can determine the path of that tennis ball based on scientific calculations. I can determine how fast it will fall, where it will fall, whether or not it will bounce, how high it will bounce, how many times and so on and so forth. It's all measureable. Therefore, I can predict an outcome and train and prepare for it.

If mysticism or magic were at play, however, I will have no idea what will happen. Therefore, not only can I not predict the outcome, but I cannot reproduce the outcome as there is nothing to calculate. My question is, if you are participating in a tennis ball bouncing competition (I believe these happen once a year and are televised on ESPN® 37 at 4am – it's riveting), which would you prefer to train with? The training style where you can calculate the outcome (reality) or the one where you have no idea where the ball is going to go every time you let go of it (mystic)? I prefer knowing that one plus one equals two rather than someone telling me one plus one equals seventy five and being given no explanation why.

Money Talks. I would like to point out a man by the name of James Randi, the founder of James Randi Educational Foundation®, JREF. He is a magician and world renowned skeptic. Specifically, for numerous years he had a standing offer of one million dollars to anyone who can prove the paranormal, such as claims of those in the martial arts using ki power. No one ever came close to winning the money. While I understand some may not be moved by money, the fact is, if they can do what they say, why not prove it, and then donate that money to charity if they don't want it?

I'm not trying to disprove these super natural powers people suggest are out there. I would love to find out they are true as it would be a truly mind opening experience. What I'm suggesting is that people spend more time on proven techniques, rather than mystical techniques that seem to have no real use beyond entertaining people during a demonstration. These proven techniques are not only just as amazing, but attainable! Your neighbor's grass only looks greener from your current perspective. Who knows, it may be covered in hidden dog poo!

CHAPTER 25

Batteries may be included, but loyalty isn't

Courtesy, Integrity, Perseverance, Self-Control, Indomitable Spirit. These are the Tenets of Taekwondo, and for the most part, tenets for most any martial artist to strive for. There seems to be something missing though. What about loyalty? It's something talked about and shown and sometimes demanded in all martial arts. So why not list it?

In my opinion, the tenets listed above are all things that the student must work on with the guidance of the instructor. Loyalty, on the other hand, is not something that only pertains to the student. Loyalty isn't, and shouldn't be given to someone just because they are in a certain position of authority. It's something that must be earned, not given. Therefore, it is something that the student and the instructor must work on together. Once loyalty is earned, it then must be maintained and built upon. Do I believe it should be a part of the tenets of Taekwondo? No. Do I think students should be quick to lose it for seemingly greener pastures? No.

I've noticed something in recent years that's been bothering me. While I believe loyalty is something that is earned and not simply given, I've seen far too many instructors, myself included, bend over backwards for students to earn the student's loyalty, only to have that student leave for perceived greener pastures. I know I speak on behalf of many of my instructor friends when I say, we all but kill ourselves for our students. Or at least have in the past. For many of us, we've watched so many students leave at the drop of a hat, making it tough to want to put forth that extra effort for a student until they've proven their worth. It's quite heartbreaking to lose those students. It's not just in their training, but on a personal level. Treating a student like family, only to watch them leave without so much as a "good bye" let alone a "thank you" is upsetting. We continue on though. We eventually learn that those few loyal students are worth every heartbreak and every ounce of pain. I have a corkboard full of thank you cards, letters, and drawings from these unforgettable students.

When I first opened my studio, it was only part time as I had another full time job. Because of that I only taught adults, knowing that teaching children was considerably more difficult. However, when I went full time with the studio, I decided it was best to open up to more ages knowing that youth students tend to be the largest base of students for most schools, and I needed to find ways to keep the doors open financially.

Two of my first youth students were brothers that I put a lot of effort into. Most days, it was just me teaching these two students. Getting to know the parents and the kids while training and traveling to tournaments, they became friends that I truly cared about, as with most of my students. The kids trained hard and built a strong base, strength and skill over the numerous months I had been teaching them. They loved class and thanked me every day for teaching them. The parents sang my praises, stating how much they have improved and how their new found skills and training have improved other elements of their lives.

One day, I took them to their first tournament a few hours away. I had planned on staying with them and just coaching them and watching them experience their first tournament. As the tournament was beginning, sadly, some of the black belts had not shown up and they were short on judges. All black belts in the building are to make themselves known when entering, as usual with these tournaments. They were short on judges and needed my help judging.

Being a black belt comes with many responsibilities, and helping judge when a fellow instructor is in need is one of those responsibilities, even if it's not what you want to do. I had to take on judging duties rather than sit with the parents and watch and cheer on my students as planned. Needless to say, the parents weren't happy with me judging, pointing out that another instructor friend of mine was not judging and was able to watch and coach his students.

Even though it wouldn't have changed anything as far as how well they did, they were upset I couldn't be there to watch all of their competitions. We talked it through and we moved past it, so I thought. Over the next year I took them to a handful of tournaments in which they did exceedingly well.

About a year and a half into their training I took them to a tournament one weekend shortly after they had received their new rank. Because of this, they had only known about half of their new form and had gotten a little rusty on their previous form as well as taking a step up in their division going into the intermediate color belt ranks. I knew they wouldn't do overly well, but they enjoyed attending tournaments, had usually done well due to their athletic ability, and I felt it was important for them to compete for the learning experience. As expected, they didn't do so well at that tournament.

The following week though, they didn't show up to class and hadn't informed me. That was rare as they came to all classes and would call if they couldn't make it. Then the next class, no students, no call. At this point I decided to call as I was worried. Worried that maybe they were in an accident on their way back from the tournament, among other worries that crossed my mind. I called a few days in a row to no avail. I grew very worried. Then about a week later, I finally got a call back. I was relieved! Until the explanation, "We decided to take our kids out of your program and enroll at another school across town."

Note that the school they took them to was my friend who was at that first tournament and it was I who introduced them. I was devastated and confused. I couldn't understand why this happened. They explained further that they felt, due to the results of the last tournament, that their training had suddenly stalled out or even regressed. This is not what happened as they were right on track with the goals I was setting for them. However, the parents didn't see it that way, they assumed that since they didn't win the last tournament, that it was my fault.

I was shocked and in disbelief. I couldn't understand why someone who constantly told me how great my training methods and results were, would suddenly leave without talking to me first. I knew exactly what was going on with their training and fully expected them to struggle at that tournament, and it was needed. They had won most every tournament they attended and I felt it was a necessary for them to struggle for a change and gain some humility, and have to deal with failure.

My fault lay in the fact that I didn't explain my process and expectations to them, though I didn't feel it was necessary since I had felt I had proven my training methods. I wasn't training them for sport and tournaments, I was using tournaments to help develop them as martial artists while I taught them self-defense, self-control, courtesy, respect, humility, etc., and not sport fighting.

For those that aren't familiar, sport martial arts and self-defense are considerably different, both in technique and in the training process. I ran over my process in my head numerous times after they left trying to figure out where I went wrong and how I could have avoided it. I felt I should have been clearer at explaining my process, or maybe I shouldn't have sent them to tournaments. I had numerous thoughts on how I could have avoided this issue. In the end, however, what I realized is that there was nothing I could have done. They would have left no matter what.

Their reasoning, whether it be the students or the parents reasoning, for training, didn't line up with my reasoning for teaching on the very first day. They didn't want what I was teaching. I just didn't know it at the time, nor did they. This event was one of the first major devastating and depressing moments of my teaching career.

I've learned from it, but the biggest thing I've learned from it is that it can't always be avoided. Every martial arts instructor has felt that heartbreak numerous times over. Supposedly less than three percent of people that train in martial arts will stick with it to black belt. That means ninety seven percent of students will quit training from their instructor, or be forced to quit. I don't care what people say, or how long someone has been teaching, it hurts every time. Every. Single. Time.

However, I've learned to not only accept the results of what happened back then, but to appreciate it. It helped me understand where I went wrong, how to avoid it to an extent, and how to deal with it when it happens. Most importantly, it helped me narrow my focus as an instructor and be straightforward with my training process. Looking back today, it was probably all for the best as it was a teaching moment for myself as an instructor and the kids fit in very well at my friend's studio. I even stopped by to watch one of them test for his black belt a couple years later and hold no ill feelings towards anyone anymore as I believe we all became better for it.

Why be loyal at all? If you feel you're not improving with your current instructor, what's the harm in leaving to train elsewhere? This is fairly common, unfortunately. At first glance, martial arts training may seem like a solo attempt at personal improvement and experience, however, it is far from it. We must rely on other students to improve. Some arts more than others, but all arts depend on other participants in order to help you train. Whether it's a partner to grapple with, or spar with, or simply give you support during a tough training day, someone else is always needed. And not just one. It's important to practice your techniques on all different body types and experience/skill levels. Not to mention, sometimes people mesh well with some and not so well with others when training.

If someone is reliant on you for their training, but you decide you want to train elsewhere, then you are affecting another person's development and training negatively. When we train, we train together as a team. Even if you don't like everyone in your class, you must learn to trust and respect them. Those who aren't trusted, respected or liked, rarely make it far in martial arts. They get weeded out pretty quickly.

Another aspect that people tend to not understand, is the process in which the body develops and refines skills. We have a saying in class, "Your only goal in class is to be better today than you were yesterday." However, there is an issue with this. We don't noticeably improve each and every day. There are ups and downs in developing new skills. You may see a big improvement when you first start your training, then you may notice a bit of a plateau, then another boost, then maybe even what seems to be a step backwards, then another boost forward. This up and down is normal and over time the downslides become less and less noticeable.

I see students hit this plateau or downslide and that's when so many jump ship. They assume this is the best time to leave or train somewhere else to get past the flat line. This effort does not work and in fact does the complete opposite. Students who jump around too often will just be avoiding the issue and will be starting over each time, never progressing or truly learning. This is where loyalty is needed. We must trust our instructors' guidance through these times. I've mentioned it in previous chapters and mention it in class regularly, you must fail and go backwards at times in order to move forward. It's inevitable.

Want a slightly complicated explanation of why we go up and down in our training? Let me put on my geek glasses for a moment and delve into the world of neuroscience. If you don't want to geek out, feel free to move past the next few paragraphs. Everything essentially comes down to two things, "Closed-Loop Motor Control" and "Open-Loop Motor Control."

When you first learn a new technique, you're going through a closed-loop program in which your brain essentially goes through trial and error to accomplish the task (the new technique.) It sends a huge number of signals to all of the muscles it believes should be involved in the technique, then uses sensory feedback to make corrections and tries it again. These sensory feedbacks could be the way it feels, the way it looks, or even outside guidance from an instructor. This process is essentially what separates a natural athlete from someone less coordinated. High level "gifted" athletes fly through this trial and error process exceedingly fast, while the average Joe may take 100x longer.

If this trial and error stops receiving sensory feedback for adjustments, it then assumes the movement is correct and turns it into an open-loop program. This open-loop program is essentially just one signal to the muscle groups involved in the technique to perform the action. When this is created, the action is essentially the same every time the signal is sent, assuming the outside forces remain the same, such as balance or forces being applied to the technique.

To help visualize this process, think of a highly detailed painting you have created that took weeks to paint. Now that you have exactly what you want in your art piece, you want all of your friends and family to have it, but instead of repainting the entire art piece every time you want to give it to someone, you simply take it to a copy machine and print off a copy to give. The process of painting the art piece would be the closed-loop program and using the copy machine would be the open-looped program.

Now, let's say you've developed this open-looped program for a front kick. Your instructor accepted the front kick as a beginner, but now that you are an intermediate rank, your instructor needs you to improve it and gives you some pointers to correct it. Maybe as a beginner you were up on your toes of your base foot and slouching over as you threw your front kick in order to get height to it. You felt it was a great kick as you were hitting targets higher than everyone else of similar rank, you feel it's your best technique!

Then your instructor pointed out these mistakes that you didn't notice. You start making the adjustments of keeping your heel down and your back straight, but notice your kick got lower, slower, and lost control suddenly. The student may see this as a step backward and get frustrated that they aren't seeing improvements as, in their mind, the improvement for your kick involved kicking even higher, faster, and with more accuracy. However, that isn't happening right away. It's easy to see why a student would feel like they aren't improving and want to seek out another instructor.

As the instructor, we see the improvement or at least know the improvement is around the corner when the adjustments are made, but the student can't always see that. To make it worse, since you now have to adjust the kick, the body removes that open-loop program and goes back to the closed-loop program, which slows down the process and can further frustrate the student.

If you trust your instructor and are loyal, you will overcome the back slide in technique and improve. This is why loyalty is so important. On a related note, this trial and error is crucial. I've seen many students think through a technique for an hour and try it once hoping they do it correctly the first time. In other fields of study, maybe this is the best approach, but not martial arts. The movement must be done numerous times over in order to perform it correctly, even if you know exactly what the technique entails and how to do it. It still won't work that first time, or first one hundred times. Trial and error, it's the only way.

On the other end of loyalty is blind loyalty in which a student stands by their instructor no matter what, even when all logic suggests this is a bad idea. I briefly trained with an association years ago that will go unnamed. I had known this association and knew it was geared towards the money more than the training, but I knew what I wanted from training there and accepted that and knew how to navigate the "we need more money from you" statement at every turn. I got what I wanted from my training there and have no regrets over it.

Being on the inside, unfortunately, was unsettling. The blind loyalty I saw from the students and the cult-like atmosphere was bone chilling. This was by no accident, mind you. The way things were set up were to isolate the students from the rest of the martial arts world. I was blatantly lied to on numerous occasions. The effort made to keep their students from experiencing outside martial arts was only surpassed by their skills of taking money from their students. It really was a cult in my mind, but I avoided drinking the Kool-Aid®, thankfully. But I digress.

I had gone to a major tournament one day with this organization and was astonished by what was going on. Before the tournament officially started, the hosting black belts lined up the one thousand plus competitors in an effort to organize everyone. They then split the competitors in half to create an aisle down the center of the very large room. They then had us chanting in order to, and I quote, "summon the spirits of the masters."

The "masters" were introduced one by one as they walked down the aisle like a politician or celebrity, shaking babies and kissing hands. Maybe the other way around, my memory isn't the best. They would eventually walk towards and sit at a head table that was raised up above everyone else where they were waited on hand and foot while eating meals and doing nothing all tournament long, except to sign an occasional autograph.

To kick off the tournament the host, I believe he was a seventh or eighth degree black belt, was to do a demonstration. He was going to do a form for his rank and a handful of board breaks. I don't recall all of the board breaks announced, but one station was a double kick and a punch. That involves jumping and doing two kicks, one with each leg, and a punch, all while in the air.

At another station was a huge contraption set up to hold ten stacked boards horizontally, with no board spacers. That's ten inches thick of solid wood! I thought to myself, if he pulls this off, I may be a convert to this cult. Not only have I never seen anyone break ten stacked boards with no spacers before, the jump kick/punch in the air is something even elite twenty year old demo team members would find daunting, and this "master" looked to be in his fifties and didn't quite look like an elite athlete.

The form he performed was forgettable. All I remember is that it was unnecessarily long and simple. But I was here to see those super human board breaks. Up first, the jump double kick with a punch! His first attempt barely left the ground, let alone get a single kick off. Second attempt, mildly better as he got one kick off that barely touched the board. He quickly turned around to the massive crowd and mentioned he was fighting through an injury and had hoped it wasn't going to affect him, but it was holding him back and needed to change the board breaks.

Now he was going to do a standing round kick on one board, a side kick on another, then a punch on the third, all standing, and one board. The same thing I make my eight year old color belts do. There was still hope as my mind would still be blown if he could break those ten stacked boards with a side kick. He broke the second station and I don't even recall what it was as it was that mundane.

Then on to the ten stacked boards. Here he goes. Thud. None broke. Second attempt. Thud, the back one broke. Third attempt. Thud, another one or two in the back broke. This went on and on about five or six more times until he broke them all, one or two at a time. I was dumbfounded. Impressed by his insanely high and unreasonable confidence in doing these board breaks in front of well over a thousand people, but dumbfounded. I busted out laughing.

Then I realized I was the only one laughing. That's when the shock, sadness and worry set in. As I looked around the room, everyone was cheering as if he just "nailed it" with all of these board breaks and made no mistakes.

This blind, unyielding loyalty was disturbing. How would this not lead students to rethinking their training with this organization? Sadly, this happens every day in every kind of organization across the globe, not just martial arts. Once someone connects with a group, they will convince themselves that they are the "good ones" and will change everything they believe in, if needed, to align their beliefs with the group.

Is the only way to show loyalty, to just keep training? No. For some students it's just not an option to keep training anymore, but I have a laundry list of black belts and past students that continue to show their loyalty to the school even without being able to continue their training. Some have helped offer free photo shoots for class photos and advertisements. Some have helped volunteer at fundraisers. Some simply keep in contact or stop by to say hello from time to time. Even my websites, and the blog that led me to writing this book, is brought to you by one of my black belts and former student. These are all examples of loyalty.

I know I can call up twenty five current or former students right now and ask them to help me with something tomorrow morning and no less than twenty three will be there without question. I know this because I've made this phone call before when I needed to move into a new studio one year and needed help moving all of the equipment over in one day. I had an army show up and moved the entire studio across town in just hours. You can't ask for better loyalty than that.

Should you be loyal no matter what? The stories above suggest that loyalty is something that needs to be addressed and reassessed from time to time. There are plenty of times where it's in your best interest to cut your ties and let go of the loyalty, even when loyalty has been built up. If it's clear the instruction you are receiving is not what you thought it was and if your goals and your instructors' goals don't line up, then it's time to move on. Ideally, this is something that should be discussed before training even begins.

As mentioned in my first story about the two students leaving, the students and their parents were interested in competition being their goal, not self-defense. If this is the case, then it must be addressed. In some cases, the instructor can adjust for the students' new goals, in other cases, they may not be able to do so, and it's best to part ways or at the very least, seek their training elsewhere.

If you feel training with your current instructor is having a negative effect on your life, it's time to go. That could mean a lot of things. It could mean that you don't feel safe training with your current instructor and need to find something safer. It could be more socially negative, such as if your instructor is involved with illegal activity or something that could affect you just by association. With that said, if you truly believe in your instructor and their actions or believe they are wrongly accused, there is a decision to be made. Point being, loyalty isn't an easy thing. It's something that needs to be worked on by everyone involved. That is the point of this chapter.

I find far too many people train selfishly. I can't tell you that is the wrong way to do it. I may disagree with it, but that doesn't mean I'm correct. A student needs to recognize it, however. For me, I take a lot into consideration when promoting a student, especially at black belt. Black belts need to give back. Give back to the school, give back to their fellow students, give back to the instructor, and give back to the community. All of these have helped them obtain their black belt. It was not a lone journey.

The school I grew up training in back in Nebraska was heavily run by the black belts just as much as the owners.

That's because the owners, my instructors, were fantastic and built loyalty from their students. The black belts taught many of the classes, set up rank testings, set up tournaments, helped get the word out about the school, helped clean, helped run introductory classes, and on and on. Most successful schools are run this way, the black belts take on a large role in making sure daily school functions are being done. Also keep in mind, training at another school or attending an outside seminar doesn't necessarily mean you are disloyal. I've encouraged my students to do so when they feel it can benefit them. All I've ever asked is for them to bring back what they learned and help make our program even better!

In conclusion, I suggest taking the time to stop and think about loyalty if you haven't already. One important element in your training should be your communication with your instructor(s). I've had students ask about their progress or bring up concerns in their training in the past and some that have changed their goals while training and needed to let me know. That never bothers me, it helps me. More often than not I can adjust things or at the very least explain the process better if there is confusion. In rare cases, I even help them get into a different school that caters better to their goals and needs if I don't feel I can meet those needs. So, take the time to build that loyalty, or take the time to think through or discuss any issues that are keeping you from it. It's an important element that most instructors are looking for when it comes to promoting and being more open to their students.

CHAPTER 26

Bully me once, shame on you, bully me twice, shame on someone else

A lot has been made of bullying over the years, bringing to attention some of the issues that many youth have to deal with. As with anything that gets brought to our attention, the issue explodes and fingers are pointed all over the place, and everyone has an opinion on how to fix it. And, well, I'm no different. Before I give my opinions on the matter, however, I find it necessary to point out what real bullying is. Much like the word terrorism is now used to describe any and all crimes committed after 9/11, the word "bullying" seems to have replaced such things as hazing, ribbing, and teasing among other things even though they are starkly different.

What is a bully? It's someone who is habitually cruel to another, to get what they want, or to simply put down another person. Yet, the word gets thrown around for just about anything these days. A child gets laughed at for having gum in their hair and it's considered bullying. I had a student one time complain that he was being bullied by another student. We'll call the accuser, "Cartman." The accused bully was the nicest kid in class. We'll call him, the accused, "Buddha." Needless to say I was baffled. I found out later that Cartman, the one crying "bully" was actually calling the Buddha, "fat." Then when Buddha called Cartman, "fat" in retaliation, he couldn't handle it and cried out, "bullying."

Retaliation isn't bullying. Not that it's good to do, but it's not bullying. Yet, despite trying to explain this to the parents, they both freaked out when they heard the word "bullying." I, subsequently, was thrown into an hour-long meeting with both sets of parents.

It also seems we've gone to great lengths to try and stop any child from saying anything negative towards another child whatsoever. But isn't that how we keep others in check? Shame? I seem to recall being a bit overbearing and controlling with some of my friends when I was younger, and not overly nice. I had no idea I was being a jerk. They told me, but I thought they were just joking with me. Then one punched me in the face a few times and I got the message, and we went back to being friends.

While there could have been numerous better ways of getting that message to me, the fact is, it worked. Shame is a great equalizer and how society tends to get people to conform without excessive violence or restrictions.

Of all the things that parents of my youth students could have concerns about when it comes to their children, the thing I hear the most is about their kids being called names or being made fun of. While these are legitimate concerns, it always ends with me finding out that the kid that was called names was being rude or cruel to the other kids, so the other children shunned or shamed that child until he/she stopped. I'm not saying I condone name calling, I don't, but kids aren't exactly masters of diplomacy. Name calling is generally their first line of stopping undesired actions of another child. My point being, this isn't bullying.

Bullying is a completely different monster and needs to be approached differently. Knowing the difference between bullying, teasing, and shaming is crucial as they come from completely different areas. A child who occasionally teases another or uses shaming in hopes to stop another's behavior just needs to be corrected and made aware that their way of dealing with issues needs to be adjusted. These are not bad kids with social disorders or issues. Bullying on the other hand can be the result of large issues at home or elsewhere that manifest themselves into bullying behavior.

What causes a child to be a bully? There are many different scenarios that cause a child to bully another. In some cases, it can be temporary, in others it can be a lifetime of this behavior. Many kids act as a bully at times throughout their childhood or as an adult. For them, simple discipline and awareness of their actions are enough for correction. A little bit of power can make anyone slip up and act as a bully at times.

Society in general tends to give more attention to those who do wrong and cause problems than those who do right. This attention, even from a bad action, is desired. It is crucial that we give just as much attention, if not more, to those who are behaving correctly. For a select few, those that tend to be engrained to bully, simple discipline isn't enough. These children tend to have much deeper issues that lead them to bullying.

For some kids, it's a lack of family involvement at home or possible abuse. This abuse or lack of affection can be passed on to their peers. Sometimes not even on purpose, there's a lack of understanding how affection and caring are shown and kids have no examples at home. For some, a "social rejection" can lead to bullying behavior, as they seek recognition and power that they are unable to attain in other forms such as good grades, sports, or popularity.

Another thing to remember is that being controlling, especially in a violent way, is how we survived throughout our history, the survival of the fittest. There was no diplomacy or asking for permission, simply doing what it takes to survive. As I've mentioned in a previous chapter, we are very violent creatures and our violence must come out in proper ways and we must be taught proper ways of dealing with others. Some suggest that exposure to violence at a young age, even as a one year old, be it real violence or on TV/games, may desensitize youth to violence.

What can be done about it? For those trying to better understand why bullying happens, we must focus on both the bully and the victim. Many studies have suggested that both bullies and victims tend to sprout from the same seed, albeit at the opposite ends of the spectrum when it comes to their actions. In many cases, both have been known to have family conflicts and have difficulty with problem solving skills in social situations. One will lash out with violence to control what they struggle with while the other pulls back and shy's away from these situations. Therefore, it stands to reason that what helps one might help the other to an extent.

Being a martial artist, obviously my answer is going to be martial arts. But what is it about martial arts that helps calm bullies and helps give confidence to victims? For starters, being a martial artist is belonging to a special group with a family-like atmosphere. What do many bullies and victims struggle with? Not having a proper functional family atmosphere, which leads them to struggle with fitting into groups.

Dan (left) with student, Roman Mijangos (middle) and visiting student, Gus Morelli (right) post sparring session to prepare for an upcoming bout. Photo by Vincent Morelli

Martial arts also teaches problem-solving skills in social situations. Students must rely on each other for progress; they must communicate, trust, and support their fellow martial artists. There's another thing that happens while in martial arts that involves learning about yourself. For bullies, they find out they can't control everyone through threats and that they aren't as tough as they thought. It tends to humble them as they start to feel the same helplessness the victims feel when they can't control a situation that makes them uncomfortable. Once they are humbled, they are brought back up. With confidence and respect they start to do the right thing and work hard, rather than resort to violence and threats. They are suddenly being recognized and rewarded for their good behavior and not recognized through punishment of bad behavior.

For the victims, they begin to see just how strong they really are. They are so used to being told how weak they are, they don't realize their strengths, and therefore have no confidence. Martial arts helps them find those strengths, as well as, strengthening their weaknesses. I'm not just talking physical here, either. For some it's their intelligence, or the creativity, or their leadership abilities.

There are numerous different ways a person can be strong. At higher ranks students are put into leadership roles in which they have to properly lead a classroom. For bullies, they learn that proper leadership is done through respect and setting good examples, not through threats and violence. For the victims they learn that they do have the strength to lead and that others do respect them when they begin to respect themselves.

I've watched numerous bullies and their victims walk into my classroom and within a reasonably short amount of time, walk out as friends. Sometimes, it happens the very first class. The power of wanting to be a part of something is huge. Both the bully and the victim walk into that martial arts studio knowing no one. Then they see a familiar face. It doesn't seem to matter that they didn't get along outside of the studio, because the devil you know is better than the devil you don't. And when you take the time to get to know someone, it's hard to not gain respect for them. We're social creatures, some of us are just terrible at being social, but that doesn't remove that urge and that need to be social, and a part of something.

What about sports? Don't sports promote much, if not all of the same confidence, social interactions, and leadership skills? Absolutely! The problem, however, is that you must be good at the sport in order for many of these aspects to work. Only the best players get playing time, or even make the team. This isn't the case in martial arts. You don't need to be the best, or even good, to build these same skills. Martial arts is about personal development, you're only competing with yourself. If you choose sports over martial arts, that's great, but it's not necessary to build these skill sets.

I'm not suggesting martial arts is the only way to help reduce the bullying that goes on. There are numerous things that can be done, in particular by families. Parents or primary caregivers must instill discipline into children and teach them right from wrong. They must tell and show them love and support while also correcting them when they step out of line.

These things, sadly, aren't being done by enough parents. We let our young children sit and watch violent movies and play violent video games and laugh when they punch and kick their older siblings or family members. Then they are shocked when their children do the same thing to children their own age and it ends in a bad way. Our society is growing increasingly dependent on other people to raise our children. Yet we drain financial resources from our schools, killing music, art, and sports programs that give an outlet to struggling youth. When a child lashes out in school, such as being a bully, nothing generally comes of it. The school may report the issue to the parents or, at best, suspend the student. This doesn't solve anything. This system of dealing with youth who are suffering with issues does not work.

Discipline and support start in the home, and then should be added to in the schools, athletics and martial arts facilities, and then brought back home in order for progress to be made. We also must focus on both the bullies and the victims, not just one. As usual, it's not just one thing that needs to be fixed, it all must be improved. We're a nation of finger pointers thinking that one thing is the problem and that one thing will be the solution, and that just isn't true. We need to let go of our sheep-like minds that only listen to our political parties or religious figures that tell us the other group is always to blame and see things for ourselves and do what we feel is best for us and our community. We are all equal cogs in the machine that makes society work, and if one part is broken, we must not blame others, we simply need to fix it. If not, it all falls apart. We can't let egos and "who's right/who's wrong" delay or distract us from the true problems and the true solutions.

CHAPTER 27

And the winner of the blame game is: No one!

Dan presenting a trophy to the winner of an annual sparring tournament.
Photo by Jen Van Kirk

It was December of 2003. I was a third degree black belt in Hapkido and had returned to training in Taekwondo to achieve my first degree black belt. This was the testing I was scheduled to earn that Taekwondo Black Belt. I was confident. Overly confident. So much so that I had told the Hapkido students I had been training to come watch me test so they could see how it was done and what was involved. No ego whatsoever going on there! I knew my form. I was confident in my sparring and I hadn't missed my board breaks, ever.

However, there was an issue. A month prior, at the national's tournament, I had torn a hamstring muscle. I was in my early twenties though, so I was clearly indestructible and it wouldn't impair me. Never mind the fact that I hadn't been able to lift my leg higher than a foot off the ground for the past month, it was just temporary pain, that black belt was forever.

First up were my forms. There were a couple of kicks with that leg in my forms. I powered through them. I kicked higher than I had kicked in a month, nearly head level. Have you ever physically heard a muscle tear and a pelvis pop out of place? It was the sound of me getting my black belt if I didn't pass out from the pain and could finish my board breaks and sparring.

I pushed through my sparring, avoiding any right leg kicks and doing more left leg and hand work. It was good enough. My board breaks though were next. I was to do a jump front kick at head level to break two boards. I had only practiced the board break with my right leg, the one with the torn hamstring, but no worries, I said to myself. I got this. My leg had stiffened up again and I had no power in it. So I decided to use my left leg.

Dan getting ready to do board breaks for a rank testing.

My first attempt, didn't break. My second attempt, as well, didn't break. This was my third and final attempt or I don't pass. Not passing wasn't an option. I was a third degree in Hapkido, I was too good to fail. On my third attempt I broke the boards! With joy and unmatched confidence, I proceeded to my back elbow board break to finish the testing and head home with another accomplishment. I wound up, threw everything I had into the boards. I didn't notice my board holders had shifted and tilted the boards too far forward and I slammed my triceps directly into the top corner of the boards, injuring my triceps and not breaking the boards. I was stunned. I was pissed. I couldn't believe the board holders cost me my black belt and made a fool out of me in front of the students I had brought to testing to "show them how it's done."

I waited for the judges to say, "Hey, let's do that again, I know we normally only do three attempts, but clearly this wasn't your fault and you deserve another try, but with better holders this time." But that response didn't come. The response was, "Bow out, and come back in a couple of months to try again."

I felt humiliated in front of the students. I thought they'd all leave believing I wasn't good enough to teach them. I was devastated. I had never failed a testing before. Clearly everything and everyone, but myself, were to blame over that failed testing. I blamed the board holders. I blamed the judges for not letting me have another chance when it clearly wasn't my fault. I even blamed the tournament I went to that led to my torn hamstring the month before. If all of these things were different, maybe I would have passed.

The blame game. The only game we play that has no winners, no prizes, and no spectators that enjoy watching. Yet, many of us play it anytime things don't go our way. It's a quick, easy way of not feeling responsible for an outcome. The issue is that it never fixes anything. If we place all the blame on someone or something else, then there is nothing we can improve or adjust to get a more desirable outcome.

After my failed testing, all I did was blame everyone else for my failed testing. If I had kept that mindset, I would have surely failed the next testing as well. Thankfully, I came to my senses and started to look at my own faults in the matter. By recognizing my own faults, I could then make adjustments to improve and make sure I didn't fail again.

The following week, returning to teach classes and expecting backlash from my failures, something unexpected happened. That testing motivated the students even more. They saw that it doesn't matter what your rank is, or who you are, you can't expect to receive your next belt just by showing up. You had to earn it. No one quit, no one thought less of me as a student or teacher. None of that happened as they were all too busy working harder to make sure they didn't fail their next testing.

There were a couple of realizations from this. First, it was one of the best things that could have happened to me. My ego was growing far too big, and it needed to be burst and deflated in order for me to progress. It was a great learning experience for me and the students to understand that you shouldn't be too confident and that you need to train heavily no matter what. I clearly slacked in my training at the time.

Second, I realized that blaming someone else for that failure was ridiculous, as I had more control over my performance than they did. I could have trained harder and practiced more with my left leg. I could have paid more attention to the boards on my elbow breaks and saw that they were tilted too far and adjusted them. I could have prepped better at the tournament by not stretching for so long. I could have gone to the chiropractor beforehand to adjust my pelvis as it was the reason I tore my hamstring. My pelvis popped during my stretches and pulled sharply on the muscle which led to the tear. Yes, there were a few things out of my control that didn't go right, but there were far more things within my control that I could have done better.

In the years since, I've dramatically altered my mindset when it comes to recognizing my own mistakes and my involvement in my failures, as well as my successes. It's easy to point the blame at another person, or situation, that leads to an undesirable outcome. It's also easy to go in the other direction and award someone else as the reason for your successes. Neither are overly accurate. The fact remains, though, that even when we include all outside sources that may impact our lives, that we ourselves, still have the most impact and involvement.

We can't ignore these outside mishaps, but we have to understand that there is little to nothing we can do about them. What we can do, though, is adjust our own actions and reactions to life's events. I see on a regular basis where students and clients have made mistakes in their training that has led to undesirable outcomes. I've had clients in the past lie to me, and themselves, about their diet or how often they exercise, only to blame me, the program, or even the science of weight loss on their lack of results. I'm sorry, but you're overweight because you ate too many calories and didn't burn enough through exercise, not because you have a slow metabolism, at the age of twenty three. And no, that martial arts technique isn't, "impossible for you because your body wasn't built that way." It's impossible for you because you haven't put in enough training time to perfect it. Yes, some have to train longer and harder than others for some techniques, but that doesn't mean it's impossible. It's just difficult. It's not meant to be easy. If it was easy, everyone would be doing it and everyone would be a black belt, or everyone would be thin, or accepted into Harvard.

It's easy to place the blame on someone or something else. It relieves us of feeling like we failed. Take it from a man who's spent more than his fair share of time blaming outside issues for his own shortcomings. It does nothing but lead you to further failure. It doesn't present solutions to problems, it doesn't make you feel better, and it doesn't adjust behavior to lead to success in the future. It only leads to frustration and anxiety over constant feelings of being out of control of the circumstances.

I leave you with a story of an incident that occurred with my youth students that I feel presents this blame game quite well, and how all future negative outcomes could have been avoided if the blame hadn't been thrown around. I let my after-school youth students have play time in which they have mostly free rein over what they do for about thirty minutes. They can decide what games they play, how they play, who they interact with, and so on.

The adults don't interject, step in, or dictate anything unless we foresee a major incident coming or an argument cannot be settled between the students. I feel it's important for this age group to deal with their own issues and test the boundaries within a safe environment in order to learn how to better interact with others and deal with problems.

The issue arose between two students. I'll call the ten-year-old "Luke" and the six-year-old "Timmy." During this play time, a group of students were playing a version of dodgeball.

Luke felt that Timmy was cheating. Luke's first reaction was to try and physically pull the ball away from Timmy due to his cheating. He pulled violently at the ball, jerking Timmy around momentarily until he let go of the ball and began to cry due to the shock of the violent nature of the older, larger Luke. Luckily, Timmy was unharmed, just shook up.

The other students scolded Luke and told him to go away while comforting Timmy. This is when we, the adults, stepped in. I showed Luke the video of what he had done through the security cameras and gave him a suitable punishment. Sadly, Luke refused to believe it was his fault and constantly blamed Timmy. Even when writing an apology letter to Timmy, as per his punishment, it was riddled with placing the blame on Timmy.

Upon reading this "apology," we had a discussion. I noted how his actions of blaming someone else and reacting poorly, not only hurt himself due to the punishment and having to tell his parents, who would also proceed to punish him, but led the other students to supporting Timmy, even though they too believed he was cheating at the time. I also stated how the entire situation could have been dramatically different if proper actions were taken.

Since most of the students partaking in the game felt that Timmy was cheating, as I explained to Luke, if he simply would have told Timmy that he was not allowed to play anymore due to his cheating, Luke could have continued on playing, not gotten punished, and Timmy would have been essentially punished by his classmates by not being allowed to play anymore. Instead, due to his knee jerk reaction, it was Luke that was punished while Timmy was comforted and supported the rest of the play time with no punishment.

Sadly, Luke still refused to stop playing the blame game, and due to this, he repeated these actions the very next week as soon as he was allowed back into playtime from his week of punishment. Since he saw no blame in himself, he never adjusted his behavior or reactions, and therefore the exact same outcome was the result. He accused yet another child of cheating, and then proceeded to push a heavy bag into the other student, and was promptly punished yet again.

Sadly, at the time of writing this, Luke still holds onto resentment and anger due to his blame of others for his punishment. Due to this constant blaming of others, he is continually punished due to his actions of anger towards those he blames while absolving himself from any wrong doing. He rarely is allowed to participate in play time, and has been held back at rank promotions more than any other student I've ever taught, all due to his behavior.

It is only with time that I hope he begins to understand the error of his ways and that seeds have been planted for future understanding, as I know it will be a very difficult and frustrating life if he doesn't realize that his tendency to blame others for his difficulties is the culprit to his suffering.

It's a lesson we all must learn, some of us learned it early on, some later on. Some will never learn, and it's quite unfortunate. Self-blame is not an easy thing to do. For many of us, it's completely against our nature to accept that we're at fault for anything. However, the sooner we can get past this uneasy feeling and the knocking down of our ego, the sooner we can make adjustments to better improve our lives.

CHAPTER 28

Ignorance breeds hate, and Lucifer breeds children's dolls

"Daniel... ," a light, slightly creepy, voice whispered from my closet in the middle of the night. I woke up. "Daniel... ," it whispered again.

Doing my best impersonation of a bad horror flick, I got out of bed and walked towards the large double door closet where one door was slightly ajar and my name was being called. I fearlessly slide the door open and looked up at the shelf that held numerous stuffed animals. All of the stuffed animals, led by an evil, yellow jump-suited knock off version of "Chucky" suddenly flew down at me all at once. They then grabbed me, lifting me up into the air and around the corner where they slammed and trapped me to the ceiling right in front of door to my room. I attempted to scream, but nothing came out. I was paralyzed with fear.

Let me back up a bit. It was Christmas time in the mid-eighties and I was about seven years old. I had unwrapped a present from my grandmother. It was a doll. Not like a Barbie®, more like a Cabbage Patch Kid® doll, but with more hair and more evil radiating from it. Yellow overalls, yellow stocking cap, thick crazy hair, and eyes that say, "I will murder you when you least expect it."

I hated that god forsaken doll. But, like the good boy I was, I smiled and said thank you. When I got home, I placed it on the top shelf with a group of hand-me-down stuffed animals, like the brown teddy bear that was missing an eye and the pretzel Velcro® doll that had its arms and legs tied in knots and stuffing coming out the sides. Don't laugh, I was grateful! None of the stuffed animals/dolls bothered me, I mostly just kept them on the shelf. The yellow demon doll on the other hand taunted me.

The first paragraph, of course, was a nightmare I had as a child. A reoccurring one in fact. I had the exact same dream numerous times over. Eventually, after a few years, I finally got rid of that banana impersonating atrocity by selling it at my grandmother's garage sale. The nightmares finally ended.

I thought I had left that poltergeist version of Raggedy Andy® behind me. Not so fast. One day, about twelve years later, I had stopped by to visit with a friend that had just returned from college. This was a friend who I didn't meet until years after I sold that demon doll. I walked into her room and instantly had a sense of dread. I looked down to my left, and there sitting on a small bench was Beelzebub reincarnated dressed in yellow.

I held back my urge to punt that evil banana with eyes across the room as not to upset my friend.

I calmly asked her, "Where did you get that doll?"

She replied, "Oh, I got that years ago at some garage sale, I loved it and had to have it!"

Apparently, she never had any horrible nightmares from the doll, nor any sense that it was going to stab her in her sleep. I was baffled. She actually loved the doll. How can this be? How can something that brought me so much suffering and hellish nightmares and paranoia, bring so much pleasure and comfort to another?

This question has plagued me for years. Why did I hate that doll so much? Why did someone else love it so much? Why do

I have one youth student that can't stand to be in class and begs his parents to quit every day, while I have another student who begs his parents to stay longer and go to more classes? Why do some people hate one martial arts style while loving another, when most martial arts teach the exact same thing and are only different in name? Why is it that many of the people I meet are vehemently against training in martial arts, yet know nothing about it?

Most of us have associations with things that subconsciously decide what we like or dislike for us, and we just go with it. That child that hates coming to class and only does so because his parents feel he needs it? Maybe it's the only time away from his parents during the day, and he hates spending time away from them? Maybe it's because it wasn't his decision and he's used to always doing what he wants and not what he's told? Maybe he's used to being rewarded without putting in effort and now he can't automatically get what he wants (his new belt) without working hard? Chances are, that child doesn't even know why he hates it, he just does and that's all that matters to him.

We all have things that bug us, or that anger us, and people we just don't like, but seemingly have no reason to feel the way we do. Do you know why you feel this way? Does holding onto this anger, fear or annoyance effect other aspects of your life? We all do this, some more than others. Most of us naturally dislike things that we aren't apart of or that challenge our comfort zone. This is what holds us back from great experiences. We associate bad things with items or experiences that we are uncertain of. It's very normal and instinctive to do so as it's a survival mechanism to an extent. We need quick ways to determine friend from foe, food from poison, pet from predator.

Like many things though, it's not needed as much anymore to make these assumptions and categories. As for that brightly colored Annabelle wannabee doll? Why did I hate it so much? Why did it give me so many nightmares, night terrors, insomnia, and sleep walking? Maybe it's because that was my first Christmas without my mother and I projected my anger onto that doll and it came out in my nightmares? Maybe it's because I watched the movie, "Childs Play" numerous times over. Maybe it's because I thought dolls were for girls and I didn't want it. Or maybe, and this is the front runner, maybe the color yellow torments me and sends me into a violent rage and murderous path. I honestly don't know, though I don't recommend sneaking up on me while wearing yellow overalls, it could end badly.

There are titles, associations, and groups throughout all of civilization that categorize us quickly. This has been discussed as an evolutionary trait and necessity in many psychology and human behavior books. A teacher, a student, a man, a woman, rich, poor, the categories are endless. While categories are useful in some regards, they can be very damaging and full of incorrect assumptions. For most people, "teacher" is associated with intelligence, educated, and wise. Yet, I could name a few that are far from all three of those traits.

At the same time, "Student" is generally seen as someone who is not as wise or educated as the teacher, and again, I've seen the opposite be true on occasion. And look no further than the news or social media to tell you exactly who all Republicans and Democrats are with no exception. Pause for eye rolls. A title or category is what we use temporarily to understand another person, place, or thing until we learn the details. Yet, this seems to be where many of us make mistakes. We seem to place someone or something into this category and never let them out, no matter what. Imagine how many relationships were passed on, experiences overlooked and knowledge bypassed all due to these incorrect assumptions leading us in another direction.

I see this categorization in martial arts quite a bit. Not just on the students' end either. It's easy to see a person stop by the studio asking about classes and immediately make assumptions that they can't afford classes or aren't going to follow through or will be a star student. I've been guilty of this many times myself. However, I've learned to try and have an open mind and not judge a book by its cover.

For students, I see them look at a technique I'm showing and I can see it on their face, "I can't possibly do that" or "That looks ridiculous, when would we ever use that?" Some move past this initial thought and learn to trust in what I'm telling them to do, some do not. Guess which ones succeed? Board breaking in martial arts is a prime example of this behavior. I'll see a student attempt to do a board break for the first time and I can see it in their eyes, "This is too hard," or "I can't break that," or "This is going to hurt."

Some push through and give it all they have and break the board, others let that board defeat them. They can smash the hand targets and heavy bags, but when they stand in front of that board, they barely tap it. The worst part is, it always hurts more when you don't break it than when you do break it. Then the "this is going to hurt" thought becomes a reality, and the downward spiral begins. This all could be avoided if the students simply believed in themselves and their instructor, and put aside their assumptions.

In this same vein of placing things into categories with assumptions, I've had many prospective students stop by my studio and ask what classes I teach. Most don't know much or anything about Hapkido or Gumdo, but when I mention Taekwondo, I sometimes get a negative reaction from that person. Sometimes, understandably, they've trained at another Taekwondo school in the past and had a bad experience. Other times, they've "heard" it's a bad art. Sadly, there are a far too many bad Taekwondo schools out there that create this assumption, but that doesn't mean they all are this way or that it has anything to do with the art itself. No matter what I say, how many facts I present, or even if by chance they let me show them how incorrect they are, they simply refuse to believe it. Once that assumption and attachment has been made, it seems to be permanent in so many minds.

Years ago, I had decided to start readjusting our Hapkido program. I moved some material around, added some things in, and started taking some things out. In particular, I removed a technique that I thought was pointless. It was a defense against a wrist grab in which you spin around, turning your back to your opponent, while grabbing their hand behind your back and torqueing their wrist to take them down.

It was a fun technique, but I thought it was ridiculous. Why would you ever choose to turn your back to an opponent just to do a wrist lock that could be applied without turning around? This seemed not only ridiculous to me, but dangerous. So I removed it. I had made an assumption, albeit a subconscious one, that whoever designed this program didn't know as much as I did, a clearly brilliant twenty something year old wannabee master martial artist.

Flash forward just a few months. I'm sparring with a student and on the ground. The student had taken my back. I couldn't see what my hands were doing. I felt his grip holding my hand behind my back. Without even thinking, I applied that very wrist lock that I thought was ridiculous and undeserving of being in the system a few months early. The student flew off my back due to the wrist lock and the position reversed.

Minutes later, I was re-editing my "new and improved" Hapkido program and putting everything back into the program that I had taken out. Not just that one defense. I had come to a realization. Not that I'm an idiot, that's a given, but that my ignorance of the reason for the technique being in the program was what led me to remove it, not my knowledge. If that was the case for one technique I removed, then maybe it's true for the others I'd removed.

Instead of completely changing everything, I turned my attention to trying to understand why a technique could be useful rather than why it was useless. This one little mental switch changed everything about my martial arts training and how I view every other technique and style. If I don't like something, or don't see why it's useful, I now assume it's due to my own ignorance and not due to it being wrong.

It's a simple change of mind. Yet, it's not so simple. The thought of it is simple, but the action and training it requires is quite complex. I still fail at this on a regular basis. The biggest difference now though is that I know I'm failing, and consciously make an effort to fail less in this regard.

How do you actively work on this mental change? For starters, try something new. Specifically, something you don't think you would like to do. Maybe you might like it, maybe you'll prove yourself correct. Either way, you won't be ignorant about the reasons anymore. Is there someone you hate? Take the time to learn about them. Take the time to hear or read about the good things, not just the bad. Why do they act the way they act? I'm a firm believer in the fact that no one is simply evil, but that their unflattering behavior was born out of necessity, or ignorance, or maybe out of their own misguided assumptions. Or maybe, you were only looking at the negative, and ignoring the positive.

One simple change I made that made a big impact, was changing my political affiliation to, "unaffiliated". I did so back in 2005 and it was quite possibly the most freeing thing I've ever done. I no longer felt the need to defend, "my guys" when they did something stupid. I soon accumulated my own ideas, thoughts, and philosophy on what I believed and how I should live my life. You wouldn't think something so simple could change so much of who you are and how you react and listen and talk to others, but it does.

Hate Taekwondo? Go sign up for some classes. Stop by my studio to train and let me show you why you may be mistaken. The point here is to allow yourself to change your mind. Rethink what you thought you knew. Look past the categories and titles we so instinctively place on people and things. Who knows, you may find out that Chucky is actually a Good Guy Doll.

CHAPTER 29

#Metoobruté?

Antje Almeida posing with a cane, a primary weapon used in Hapkido, during a photo shoot by photographer Evan Scott

I've been teaching women's self-defense courses since the late nineties. My courses have evolved over the years moving from heavy physical defense content to more awareness and prevention content. I was noticing a trend of ladies taking one course and then never training again. It worried me that I was giving these women a false sense of security, believing they can perform these physical defenses despite only briefly training them. Despite my pleas during the course telling them they need to continue to practice regularly, it just wasn't happening.

As I made my adjustments and provided more awareness and prevention content to the program, I noticed the boredom level of the class escalated, and therefore added some more physical content back in. Over the years, the attendance for these classes has been abysmal at best. I've adjusted the cost, even doing it for free, as well as adjusting the length of the course or spreading it out over multiple classes. Sadly, nothing I've done has improved attendance for these classes.

Participants have expressed their love of the classes and how much they've learned from it, but nonetheless, I've never felt it was as successful as it could be. I was also confused as to why so few women turn out to these courses. We hear the grotesque stats every day about how often women are assaulted or harassed or taken advantage of. Yet, it's a struggle to reach these ladies and teach them how to combat these stats and feel more empowered.

A few years back, I attempted to reach out to women's shelters, among other organizations that help abused women and children. To my astonishment, most rejected my efforts to teach their staff or visitors, even when I offered it for free. When I asked why they would turn down an offer, I was given a confusing answer at the time.

"We don't want these women to feel like it's their fault these things have happened to them, and therefore not their responsibility to learn self-protection."

I was stunned. I couldn't believe someone would turn down options to help improve their life and prevent further abuse and harassment. I all but gave up trying. That response stuck in my head, however, and began turning the hamster wheel I loosely call a brain. As frustrated and perplexed as I was that someone would turn down free efforts to improve people's lives, I couldn't help but agree with their reasoning. This was not their fault, it was the abuser, the men that created the issue. Therefore, why is it not the men that should be trained? This thought persisted.

Recall the last romantic love story you read or watched. The guy pined over the woman. The woman didn't recognize or want the man at the onset of the story. The guy persisted and eventually won over the woman. They are now living happily ever after. Sounds great, right? Except that these aren't love stories, they're handbooks on how to be a stalker, and win.

Our culture in this country (I'm sure it's elsewhere, but I haven't lived elsewhere) is horrific when it comes to the courtship, relationships, and general interaction between men and women. For men, we are taught not to take "No" for an answer and to be that aggressive alpha male who takes what they want rather than accepting failure and moving on.

We're taught that giving compliments and saying, "I love you" is how you get what you want from a women, rather than saying it because you believe it. Women are taught to not show interest right away and to make the guy figuratively jump through hoops to win them over, further solidifying our understanding that the word, "No" is only temporary. We're taught to follow our hearts, except that we sometimes misunderstand what our "heart" is saying. We may have a gut feeling that we interpret as, "This is love!" when it's actually trying to yell out, "Run away, be cautious!"

We're taught that men have a role and women have their role. In the not so distant past, a marriage wasn't so much of an equal loving relationship as it was an ownership of a women by a man. Thankfully, some of these things have evolved over the years, usually due to necessity or lack thereof.

For instance, when I was younger, my family used to have dinner at my grandmother's house for all of the major holidays. I recall her stating that years ago, the women would cook the meals, then call the men in to eat and serve them while not eating themselves until after the men were done. They would then clean the table and do the dishes and the men just ate. While this sounds horrifically sexist and wrong, there was a necessity for it. The men were out working on the farm all day long while the women kept the house. This was the most efficient way to live and work at the time for them. When the farm was sold, this tradition mostly ended. My grandmother still did most all of the cooking, but occasionally the men would help out, the kids would set the table and we would all enjoy dinner together, then both the men and the women would clean up. It became more efficient to do it this way now, hence the change.

Our culture has held on to many traditions like this and others, even though it's no longer efficient, needed or even desired and in some cases, dreadfully damaging to us all. That's tradition for you though, it remains the same until someone realizes it's not needed anymore. Then comes the task of convincing everyone it's not needed. Then the act of changing. That's an excruciatingly slow, tough process and there will always be holdouts that refuse to change. However, until we recognize both the problem and the solution, there is no change at all. We're at the point in our history where we recognize the problem, but seemingly no one with a voice has the answer. A lot of talking but no real action behind anything aside from anger and retaliation. Those with the answer rarely have a loud voice to be heard.

You may have noticed throughout reading this chapter that I've been stating men as the abusers and not women. Obviously, women can also be abusers. I've been a victim of harassment from women in the past. I've had women grab me without my permission in sexual ways or make uncomfortable statements. However, there is a serious difference that must be understood, specifically when it comes to harassment. At no point have I ever felt like my life or job was threatened or that I was completely out of control. Essentially, there was no fear involved, only discomfort. That is a huge difference between the two scenarios.

I've heard far too many stories from women in my classes and courses over the years that have suffered fear from harassment, stalking, mental, and physical abuse. This fear has affected their lives in negative ways and lingers on well after the initial abuse. While that's not to say it's never a two way street, the vast majority of the time, men don't have that same sense of fear when these issues come up. No fear, no ongoing stress from it, no change of behavior to avoid future harassment. We have to recognize the difference when the exact same scenarios are placed on different people.

I, as a straight white male, have never felt fearful just because of who I am, what I'm wearing or what I look like or who I'm attracted to. It's simply not a two way street when it comes to harassment. Actual abuse, on the other hand, goes both ways and something that should not be overlooked, or taken lightly, when it comes to women being abusive towards men.

What are we to do? We can keep beating our heads against the wall doing the same thing that's never worked in the past and keep seeing the exact same pathetic results as it doesn't actually solve the problem. Or we can demand a cultural change that will be fought tooth and nail for many years, but can be fought by each one of us right here, right now, without government or police involvement.

In recent years I've opened up many of my self-defense seminars to men and women, rather than just women. I've addressed men directly in these classes, explaining they need to change. To no surprise at all to me, most men had no idea they were creating such unfortunate circumstances due to their actions. In regards to this teaching men how to act, I've been somewhat vocal to anyone willing to listen about my dislike of how we educate our youth. There's this assumption that basic life skills, such as courtesy, integrity, how to (insert any basic life skill all should know, such as cooking or changing a tire) are taught in the home and not the schools' responsibility. I get it. It should be that way. The fact is though, it rarely is.

There is a complete lack of life skills being taught to youth these days. I teach it in my youth classes, in regards to behavior and personal responsibility, but I seem to be the only one if it's not taught at home. I feel strongly that human interaction and general life skills should be taught in our schools. Teaching a child how to be respectful towards each other and how to properly court someone you're interested in would have a dramatically positive impact on our society and lower these horrific cases of harassment, abuse, and even bullying.

It's highly unlikely for that to happen anytime soon and we can't wait for someone else to get it done. Therefore, it's on us to make these changes. While I can't list and explain everything that needs to be addressed and changed, I can give a few examples of what I go over in my self-defense courses that will provide a general idea of what needs to be adjusted.

Please note this is just the tip of the iceberg of what needs to be understood and changed. If you would like to see a larger list of what is listed below and read a great book on awareness and prevention, read *The Gift of Fear* by Gavin De Becker. I personally believe it should be mandatory reading for teenagers.

Refusing to accept the word, "No." This is one of, if not the biggest, issues on the list. We've been taught all of our lives that, "No" is just the start of a negotiation. Both in relationships and in business. In relationships, or attempts at them, we are taught to change that "No" to a "Yes" rather than to accept it. This holds true in business as well. Every business book I've ever read and every business seminar I've attended and every business meeting/training class I've ever been in has stated very clearly that, "No" is not an acceptable answer. You must find why the word is currently "No" and how to give a counter argument to change it to a "Yes."

The same tactics used in business are being applied to manipulating relationships. This is why I say it's a cultural thing, it's everywhere. Understand that part of this issue is the other side of this. We have a tendency to say no to things out of a reactionary response rather than it being truly our answer as we know it's a negotiation.

Stalking. While this one should be obvious to both men and women, I'm constantly surprised how many men don't know that what they are doing is considered stalking. While I don't want to incriminate a friend, I did have someone bring to my attention in the past that a friend of mine was stalking his ex-girlfriend. When it was brought to his attention, he was shocked to know that what he was doing was wrong and immediately stopped. How do we know the difference between stalking someone and simply ogling someone from afar?

It's fairly straight forward, being infatuated with someone from afar is temporary until you get up the nerve to talk to the person. Stalking is long term and involves planning and scheduling times to encounter the desired person, even when they've stated or suggested it makes them uncomfortable. Another example of inappropriately surveilling a partner involves perusing through personal stuff such as emails, texts, journals and anything else that one would consider to be private. The only acceptable reason to search through this stuff is when the person gives you permission.

Unwilling to accept change and faults of oneself. No one likes a person who is close minded and unwilling to recognize their own faults. Look at things from the other person's point of view for starters. Listen to what others are telling you and accept that this inflexibility is hurting both you and others. So few people know how to actually listen these days. Instead, we wait until it's our turn to talk. This must change.

Comparing oneself to violent people in the news or believing violence of others is justified. Men, much more so than women, have this tendency to try and act tough and popularize violence. This too is very much a cultural thing, and it seems to be growing. I don't know if it's because they think it's cool or because they feel its taboo or if they, for some reason, really enjoy violence. I honestly don't know what it is, but it needs to be understood as I feel it's one of the reasons that so many mass shootings are performed by men (I use that term, "men" loosely, very loosely.) The growing number of people that sympathize with former or current dictators of the world and violent story book characters is alarming and needs to be addressed and better understood. Ask yourself, is this you? If so, ask why. I can't imagine how worried or fearful your friends, spouse or significant other would be if they heard you saying that killing other people is a good thing.

Blaming others and refusing to take responsibilities for one's own actions. As I mentioned in Chapter 27, *And the Winner of the Blame Game is...No One!*, this constant blaming of others for your own faults and failures is a quick way to alienate yourself and send you down a road that could result in your abuse towards others you deem as the ones to blame. While this issue alone doesn't lead directly to harassment or abuse, being coupled with the previous issue of justifying violent behavior is a recipe for disaster.

Weapon love. We get it, you love the second amendment and love your guns. But do you really need to tell everyone about it? I see nothing wrong with owning a gun or any other weapon. I highly recommend it if you are highly trained, but when you talk about it constantly as if to compensate for something else that may be lacking, it becomes a giant red flag that suggests you'd really like to use it. How safe do you think those closest to you feel when they believe you're trigger happy? Stop telling people about it. It's there to help you defend yourself, not create fear in all of those around you that don't seek to harm you. Besides, isn't telling everyone you have a gun working against you? If I was looking to rob a joint, I'd take you out before trying to rob the place knowing that you're carrying, not that I would do that, but you get what I'm saying.

The Loan Shark. This is the act of doing something for someone with the intent of making them feel indebted to you. It could be something as simple as helping someone with carrying their grocery bags to the car before asking for their number. For the most part, this can be quite harmless and just a simple act of showing you are kind hearted or nice. However, the intent behind it could be considered manipulation if the only reason you did it was to get something in return. Think through your true intent behind your actions. Why are you really doing this kind act? Would you do it for everyone? Or just the good-looking blonde with the great legs, and as soon as you get what you want the kindness ends?

On a related note, no she doesn't owe you anything for that meal you bought her. As a single man, I know all too well someone going out with you only for the free meal. It's awful. However, that doesn't mean she owes you anything. I don't care that she ordered the lobster and the most expensive wine on the menu. I'll reiterate, she doesn't owe you. I've since changed to doing nothing but coffee dates to save my bank account and eliminate those who only want to get a free meal. I suggest you do the same rather than demanding something physical in return. This too is a form of "Loan Sharking."

I want to leave you with a two rules of thumb on how to gauge your actions when it comes to how to treat another human being. The first is known as the golden rule. It simply states, "Do unto others as you would want done unto you."

Don't like people stalking you? Then don't do it to someone else. Don't like being talked down to? Then don't do it to others. It's a pretty simple concept and not hard to follow. It just takes thinking before doing. The second rule of thumb is the rule of opposites. This too is outlined in *The Gift of Fear*.

Simply, it states that if you think about the actions you are making and look at the opposite of that action, you should be able to clearly see if what you are doing is right or wrong. Here are a few examples:

If someone is being intrusive and asking many unnecessary questions, look at the opposite. The opposite would be someone who is respectful of privacy and only asks necessary questions. Is a person yelling and screaming their opinions at you? The opposite would be someone calmly discussing their opinions with you.

As you can see, when you list the opposite of what you are doing, the answer of how to act smacks you right in the face!

To conclude, let me make a few things clear. While this chapter focuses a lot on opening men's eyes to our mistakes, the general message is that we need to change our culture across the board, men and women. Being a man, I know what men need to change. While I've claimed numerous times to friends that I'm a lesbian trapped in a man's body, I really don't feel like I'm in a position to tell women how to change and adjust what they do. So I'll leave the female readers to discover for themselves what needs to be changed as I'm sure there are a few things that can be done to help lower harassment and abuse.

The one thing I can suggest to women is to attend ongoing self-defense seminars or a regular martial arts program. I can't stress enough how dramatically this can change and empower one's own life, no matter your gender or age. The most common responses I get from people that don't take classes are, "I can't afford it" or "I don't have the time." Sorry, but we both know that's not true and just an excuse. Take an honest look at your expenses/income and schedule. For ninety five percent of people, you'll find ways to make it work. Treat this training as you would treat eating and sleep, and you'll find the time and money you need to attend.

I don't know what, if any, change this will bring as most of us will read this and move right along without thought. It's much easier to wait for someone else or authority figures to take the lead and make changes. I implore you though, if you want change, it has to come from you. The change has to start with a discussion, which I feel is slowly happening in the world at this moment, but the discussion must be towards the answers and corrections, not just at who is to blame.

As I mentioned above, what I have listed here is just the tip of the iceberg. We need to have discussions and actions to change our ways. We can change much of this on our own in our daily lives and ask others to do as well. It's the only way things can be changed without complicated and ridiculous laws and policies that will undoubtedly lead to frustration and political strife, as with seemingly any issue that comes up these days. So, let's make the change on our level, no one else's. It's time to be better humans towards one another.

CHAPTER 30

The trashcan pooper incident and other crappy situations

Class photo of Dan's after school program students, chaos version.

Photo by Sata Bun

It was my second year of running an after-school program, and it was a very stressful year. Hands down the toughest year of being in business. I had a few kids that were difficult to deal with and little to no help. One day, I walked into the bathroom and immediately smelled something bad. I pinpointed that it was coming from the trashcan and assumed there was some food left in there over the weekend that had rotted. Mind you, at this time, I couldn't afford a dumpster, so I put all trash in my car and drove it home.

A few days later, I walked into the bathroom and, yet again, smelled something awful. Again, I took the trash home to place in my home dumpster. The following week, you guessed it, I once again walked into the bathroom and smelled something dreadful. This time I looked through the trash a bit noticing, what I told myself, was a chunk of chocolate thrown in the trash. This trash too, I took home.

A few days later, again, an eye watering smell sucker-punched me in the face. This time, there was no mistaking it. There was a giant turd sitting front and center in the trash can. Stop laughing. It was horrific and traumatic! I still see that corny, blackened, turd staring back at me in my nightmares!

Back to the story at hand. I had to find out who was doing this vicious atrocity. So, I proceeded to inspect the bathroom after every student exited. Sure enough, I found the culprit, I found the trashcan pooper. To protect this child, I will change his name to "Lucifer." When I confronted Lucifer, he denied it at first. Upon presenting the evidence and proof, he just smirked and looked away. I asked, "Why?!" but he didn't want to answer.

With some poking and some prodding, I discovered the issue. I had been hit with a three hundred dollar plumbing bill from my landlord who claimed one of the tenants in the building flushed paper towels down the toilet and clogged everything. Therefore, to avoid more expensive plumbing bills, I put up a sign in the bathroom saying not to flush paper towels down the toilet. FYI - this same sign remains over one of the toilets at my studio to this day.

This student, Lucifer, mistook paper towels as toilet paper on the sign and assumed he wasn't supposed to flush toilet paper down the toilet. So he started off by throwing the used toilet paper in the trash. Eventually, he got tired of it and just started dropping deuces in the trashcan out of defiance.

During that same school year, as I mentioned, it was a soul crushing year, I began noticing wet spots every so often throughout the studio. In the corner in the back room. In a dressing room. On the floor of the bathroom. Even in the lobby! All of which, when cleaning it up, didn't seem to be water. Then I spotted a puddle in the trashcan. Then the plunger was filled, capped, and turn upside down. When I lifted the plunger, the liquid poured out all over the place.

It was clear a child was urinating all over the place and getting more and more creative and sinister. After doing some research and talking to some parents, the culprit was found, but not without his most sinister peeing plan already in process. Again, to protect the child, we shall call him "Satan's Little Helper." I discovered he had an issue with washing his hands.

In his mind, Satan's Little Helper had to wash his hands because he touched the flusher on the toilet, not because he went to the bathroom. Therefore, if he didn't pee in the toilet, then he didn't have to touch the flusher, and in turn didn't have to wash his hands. After sitting down and having a discussion on how his logic was slightly massively misguided, he understood that he needed to pee in the toilet, wash his hands, and to stop peeing in random places. Issue solved.

I washed my hands in victory, only to wonder why the soap suddenly had a strange smell, and was excessively frothy. Satan's Little Helper's last victim was the soap dispenser and the numerous people who had used it over the past week.

The common thread between these stories is a lack of communication or miscommunication. So many issues arise due to a lack of communication skills in all areas of life, and martial arts is no different. I've learned to adjust the way I speak over the years depending on if I'm teaching children, teens, adults, etc., in order to communicate more effectively. While they don't usually lead to poop in the trashcan or pee in the hand soap dispenser, it can impair ones training considerably.

I once had a student who kept forgetting to pivot his foot to the outside before one of his kicks. I would look at his material and the first critique I had for him every time was, "Make sure and turn your foot outward for that kick." His response was always, "Yes Sir." Class after class I would look at his kick and every time I'd start by telling him the exact same thing about turning his foot outward. This was always replied with an acknowledging, "Yes Sir."

After about two months of this, and me getting frustrated that he clearly wasn't even trying to fix the problem, I finally asked, "Why aren't you turning your foot outward? I've mentioned it every class for months now, but no adjustment. Why?" His response was, "I thought I was."

I was baffled. Upon further explaining and digging into the issue, I discovered he thought I was talking about his kicking foot while I was speaking about his base foot. After a short laugh and a sigh of relief that this student wasn't hopeless or purposefully ignoring me, I thought about how I could clarify this for future teaching. Since then, I've simply used the word, "pivot" instead of "turn."

For adults, this makes more sense that it would be the base foot as you cannot pivot a foot off the ground. However, I discovered shortly after, that this doesn't work for children as many don't know what the word "Pivot" means. So I had to go back to the word, "Turn" but with further information that included pointing towards or even touching their base foot.

After over twenty years of teaching I'm still discovering new ways to better explain and communicate to my students, knowing that all age groups come with a different set of instructions on how to speak to and teach them. Even when I feel I've made things extremely clear, I've still noticed miscommunication. I can't count how many times I've repeated a statement to a student, such as,

"In this situation, ALWAYS step to the left, never to the right," only to hear that student talk to another person and say,

"My instructor says to ALWAYS step to the right in this situation and never to the left."

In which case I face palm and walk away. I'm certain I have people who don't know me that think I'm the worst instructor ever because of situations like this, hah!

As an instructor, one of the most frustrating things to deal with is watching a student leave and not know why. Were they upset with something? Did they not feel like they were getting what they wanted? Is there another student in class causing them problems? Can they no longer afford classes? Did their work schedule change? Many of these things can be dealt with, if we just knew about them. Always communicate with your instructor or trainer or coach when issues arise. Far too many times I've watched a student or client leave due to an issue that could've easily been fixed. If we don't know about it, we can't fix it. Yes, it's not always a comfortable discussion telling someone they are failing you to the point of wanting to leave, but most instructors I know can take it.

Many times I've found that the issue was just a misunderstanding, other times it was something that was easily fixed. Occasionally, there was nothing that could be done, but at least there was some closure and understanding of what could lead to future issues with other students. I've made numerous changes to my system, payment options, schedule, etc., after listening to what students had to say. It's critical for us to know if something is working well, so please, tell us!

While there are many things that can be done to help improve communication, I've narrowed down a handful of things that I hope will help, as they have helped me over the years. Mind you, this isn't just related to martial arts, but to any time you want to communicate information to someone or learn from someone.

Active listening. Many people don't listen well, and only wait for their turn to speak or interject. Interject by asking a question rather than a comment. However, in a class setting, make sure it's a reasonable question worth interrupting. Despite what we were told growing up, there are such things as stupid questions.

Essentially, if answering the question will gain you nothing, then don't ask it. This sounds obvious, but I hear questions that people ask in which it's clear they already know the answer or they are, in their mind, politely asking a question to undermine what you are teaching. Such as the impertinent, "What if" question that is clearly asked in the tone of, "I don't think this works because my past instructor said something different." If you truly have a question though, ask it, as there's a good chance others have the same question.

Get to the point. This is one I still struggle with as I'm a storyteller. I like to set up the "punch line" so to speak. I get interrupted many times before I get to the point by those who couldn't wait any longer. I'm the guy who sends multiple paragraphs through text. And since I refuse to bastardize the English language by typing "U" instead of "you" or by removing punctuation, it's a safe bet my text will take many finger scrolls to finish.

Unfortunately, this can lead to burying the real message and leaving the listener confused. However, too little information can also be an issue, so there is a fine line to walk. Get the point across and let their questions clarify the rest.

The rule of three. As an instructor critiquing a student, I live by the rule of three. As in, give no more than three things to work on (or three points of interest). Anything more than that and the listener is most likely going to forget. Some students can handle more, some less, but I always start with three and adjust from there. I'm certain this pertains to all information given to someone who isn't writing down or recording the conversation. Oh, and ignore the fact that I have listed six points of interest in this chapter rather than three. Refer to number two for the reasons why.

Repeat back and clarify. This is especially the case for my youth students. I have them repeat back to me what I just told them so that I know they both listened and understood what I said. I've found many times that I would tell a youth student something to adjust, give them time to adjust it while working with other students, then when I come back they haven't fixed a thing. I come to find out, they completely forgot everything I told them the second I left. So having them repeat back what was told of them has proven quite valuable. I've found myself doing the same thing on the other end knowing that my memory isn't exactly stellar.

Avoid escalation. This isn't just a good idea for communication, but a good idea for self-protection. Far too many simple arguments turn violent due to escalation. We have this tendency to want to be "above" the person we are arguing with or to prove we are right and they are wrong. They say something that is rude to us or attacks our being in some way. So in turn, we do the same in retaliation, but with a harsher statement or a louder voice. Then in turn, the other person does the same thing. Eventually, your voice and quick wit will hit a cap and you result to slinging fists instead of insults.

All of this can be avoided if you just stop caring about being insulted or defending your ego, and just let the other person be, "above" you. Let them get the last (or ideally, the only) insult in. Who cares? No one. But your face might when you can't keep it closed and it gets closed for you. Let it go! Perfect your de-escalation techniques, your face will thank you.

Never say always or never. This is one the kids have forced me to learn. There's many a time where I've said, "We'll never do that" as I generalize a statement. And, of course, the kids will remember the word never more than any other word and call me out on it when we state an exception weeks later. I still catch myself about to say always or never, then quickly back it up and re-word my statement. Generally speaking, don't speak in generalities. Be precise and don't exaggerate. Be as specific and precise as possible when communicating.

Words can be powerful. They can paint a picture, they can infuse emotion, move markets, start wars, educate, or simply put a smile on someone's face. However, communication, while we all do it, can be quite difficult. Perfect your words, your gestures, your tone, and you'll cleanly pass along your thoughts, ideas and information with as little misinformation as possible.

CHAPTER 31

No pride in prejudice

"My mind is made up, don't confuse me with facts."

This seems to be the battle cry of our nation. I couldn't find who this exact quote was attributed to, as it seems to be uttered by, sadly, far too many people. Let's be honest, we all have followed this quote, even if we didn't verbalize it. Our parents, friends, pastors, neighbors, political parties, etc., all help shape our opinions on what to believe, what is good and what is bad. The issue is that we forget to question these opinions as we blindly trust these individuals and groups.

To make matters worse, with the advent of the internet and social media, we have connected with more like-minded individuals throughout the world and, with little to no resistance, have accepted their thoughts and opinions as fact. And now, far too many people believe the world is flat. Yes, a growing number of people truly believe that. And, of course, the martial arts are no exception.

The misinformation, myths, and misconceptions in martial arts are mind boggling. Moreover, even when people have the truth bluntly punched in their nose, they still refuse to open their minds. When I was in the third grade, my brothers gifted me, The Simpsons Sing the Blues cassette tape for Christmas. Shut up, it was awesome! Remember, I was in the third grade and the Simpsons® were huge. Don't judge me if I happen to still have it in my music rotation. Also, don't judge me that I still have a cassette player. Anyway, in the insert of the cassette, which provides album information, there was a name and a picture of each of the main characters and the people who voiced them.

To my shocking surprise, Bart Simpson was voiced by a woman, Nancy Cartwright. My mind was blown! The foulmouthed cartoon boy I looked up to was actually a woman?! I could hardly believe it, but there it was, in print. I, of course, did what any third grader would do when their world gets flipped upside down, I told all of my friends. One by one, they didn't believe me. Not only did they refuse to believe me, they all stopped being friends with me, stating I was lying and trying to talk smack about the Simpsons. Sadly, and pathetically, I never really gained those friends back. We became friendlier over the years, but nowhere near as close as we once were. This was all because they were convinced that Bart Simpson was voiced by a man and refused to believe otherwise. It took me having to bring the cassette in to school to show them the proof. Even then, they held it against me that I shattered their world. It just goes to show how deep our beliefs are and how resistant we are to change if we don't like it or if it proves us wrong.

I first started my martial arts journey in October 1994. My oldest brother signed us both up with the intention of doing Hapkido. Neither of us had any idea what Hapkido was. All I had heard of were the basics, Karate and Kung fu, and recognized the name of Taekwondo but knew nothing of it. We briefly watched the Hapkido class and were instantly in love. We had never seen grappling, throws, joint locks, ground techniques, and pressure points before. We had only known of the kicks and strikes we saw from the movies. We were sold.

There was, however, an issue. The only students in the class were law enforcement and I had to be at least sixteen. I was only thirteen. My older brother was allowed in, but the instructor said I could train in Taekwondo instead until I was old enough. I begrudgingly accepted, and then secretly trained Hapkido at home with my brother. Shush, don't tell my instructor. Even while training in Taekwondo, I was focused more on Hapkido. I didn't hate Taekwondo, I rather enjoyed it, I just didn't respect it the way I should have. I felt, and had convinced myself, that Hapkido was the better art and Taekwondo was for those who couldn't do Hapkido, whether due to age requirements, physical limitations, or intimidation.

The longer I trained in Taekwondo, however, the more I began to respect it. Yet, I never put as much focus or effort into it as I did for Hapkido. After over a year of training in Taekwondo, my instructor noticed my maturity in class and sought out, and obtained, permission from his instructor to allow me to begin training in Hapkido just before my fifteenth birthday. I was thrilled, I was pumped, I was psyched. I was in a lot of pain that first week of Hapkido as I got pummeled on by large adult law enforcement that seemed to know nothing less than full force against my fifteen-year-old, 125 pound frame. All I can say is that I loved it!

I also, unfortunately, quit Taekwondo. Again, I enjoyed it, but I just didn't think it had anything to offer over Hapkido. The problem was, I had come to that conclusion before I even started Taekwondo. I didn't return to Taekwondo until numerous years later when I reached my third Degree in

Hapkido. I foresaw myself moving away in the near future and wanted to obtain my black belt in Taekwondo before leaving so that I could begin teaching Taekwondo, as well as Hapkido, when I relocated.

Flash forward another few years, where I discovered and researched more about Taekwondo and its origins. I finally began to understand the science and power of Taekwondo. Over the years and actively researching, discussing, and training with great Taekwondo practitioners, my respect and love for Taekwondo began to grow immensely. It took too long for me to respect and love Taekwondo. The frustrating part is that it was my own fault that I held back truly learning the art. I can't help but wonder how much farther along I'd be in my training if I was more open minded. Not just in my Taekwondo training, but my Hapkido training as well.

There are numerous techniques in Hapkido that are greatly improved when you add the Taekwondo philosophy of sine wave, a form of power generation, to them. I've made it a point to never judge a martial art or even a school or instructor until I've thoroughly experienced them. That open mindedness has led me to many different seminars and classes in which I've learned a great deal of technique and thoughts from other styles and instructors that have massively improved my own programs with Hapkido, Taekwondo, and Gumdo.

Chances are, if you know at least a little about martial arts, and are not a Taekwondo practitioner, just reading the name, "Taekwondo" made you roll your eyes. I've received numerous emails and phone calls asking about my classes that have consisted of scoffing at Taekwondo. Yet when asked if they have ever studied Taekwondo, the answer is either, "No" or "briefly years ago." It's clear to me that so much certainty in their decision is based on little knowledge and experience.

This assumption that a style is bad or ineffective, no matter what the style, is ignorant. If you've taken martial arts, or have had a discussion based on martial arts, chances are you've heard the question, or someone's opinionated answer of, "What style of martial arts is best?" I've heard a hundred answers to this pointless question. Usually it depends on what art is currently popular based on a recent movie, a new style being introduced into the Olympics®, or as is the case in recent years, the UFC™ and other MMA sport fighting promotions popularizing a few other styles.

Many folks who are long time practitioners and study many arts will tell you it's not the style but the teacher and/or the student. This is definitely true as all styles have their merit. However, there was an answer to this question I heard years ago, though I don't recall who stated it. His response was, "each martial arts style is best for what it was created for." I thought this was a brilliant answer to a difficult question.

If you look through the history of each style, you'll see in most cases that there is a reason why it came about. Not just because someone was bored and decided it would be cool to make a new style. Though I'm sure there are plenty of people that have gone that route, but not likely those styles that are well known. Some styles came about due to a need for physical self-defense. Some were created as sport. Some are geared towards physical or mental wellness.

Take Taekwondo for instance. My apologies for the bastardized history lesson about to be given to those who may dislike it: While there are numerous different Taekwondo organizations, it can be broken down into three major branches: International Taekwon-Do Federation (ITF), World Taekwondo Federation (WT-formerly WTF-you can understand why they changed the name) and American Taekwondo Association (ATA). Many folks don't realize that it is a very modern martial art, officially named in 1955. Looking back at history provides some insight. Korea had just gone through some serious wars, including the Korean War which is known as the Forgotten War. In the aftermath, and the divide between North and South Korea, many felt as if they had lost their identity. South Korea looked to a group of martial artists, led by General Choi, to develop a self-defense system for their military, and eventually, their country. General Choi, mind you, was a very small individual, so the art of Taekwondo was built very scientifically to overcome strength issues when defending oneself.

The Taekwondo founders even took to the universities to make use of, at the time, the latest technology to refine the techniques for power and efficiency. It was also used as a way to bring South Korea together as a country, so the art is littered with history and iconic figures from Korean history. Korea and its history were nearly wiped off the earth during the war, and the Japanese occupation, and they didn't want that to happen again. Now, Taekwondo is the most practiced martial art in the world.

It's safe to say, the world will not forget or lose the rich history of Korea ever again due to this! In 1969, the ATA was formed as a separate form of Taekwondo that catered more to the "flashier" kicks of Taekwondo, which appealed to a wider range of practitioners who may have been bored with the heavier training of the basics in the lower ranks, where many students quit. The ATA also took a step closer to catering to the sport aspect of Taekwondo.

Then, in 1973, The WT was created as an alternate version of Taekwondo to the original Taekwondo (which become the ITF) after the South Korean government ousted General Choi for his allowing of Taekwondo to be taught in North Korea. The WT went the route of sport with the hopes of being accepted into the Olympics to help more widely spread the name and art, which it successfully did as it's now the official sport of South Korea. The point of this bastardized history lesson of Taekwondo is to point out that even within one martial art style, there can be many different variations. From self-defense to sport to "flash." This is why when I hear a potential student scoff at Taekwondo when I mention it being a great art for self-defense, I have to assume they've learned about Taekwondo through the flashier versions or sport versions that don't cater as much to the self-defense portion of the art or have studied from an instructor who received their black belt online or through an "advanced" 1 year version, which is degrading to the art.

In addition, I'm less likely to take that person on as a student knowing that if they're so closed-minded about a martial art, then I don't really want to deal with that same closed-mindedness throughout class. The important thing to know when trying to find a martial arts style that is best for you, is to know what it is you want to get from the art you want to train. Then ask questions to area instructors and practitioners. Research what a style is all about and how it came about, not just watching poorly done videos of demos that don't really demonstrate the art more than it tries to spice things up to get people interested. There is ten times more misinformation out there than there is proper information. Take the time to educate yourself before making a decision, not just when it comes to martial arts, but in all of life. And as mentioned above, the instructor has more to do with the success of your goals than the art being practiced.

Understand that trusting certain individuals, such as the ones listed at the onset of this chapter, is critical for efficient navigation through life. However, properly timed questioning of everything you know is essential to positive change and self-improvement. They say that eighty percent of what we know in life is learned before we are seven years old. Our world is shaped in seven short years before we close our minds to anything new and let go of learning. Let's collectively work to lower that eighty percent to seventy five percent! One step at a time, got to be realistic. Now go learn something!

CHAPTER 32

The only rule necessary for mankind:
Don't be a jerk

Two adult black belt competitors sparring at a tournament.

When I first started my after-school martial arts program, there were a lot of elements I had to figure out. I knew how to teach martial arts, but scheduling for snack time, study time, and play time, was complicated. Play time was a big question mark for me as I didn't know how to approach it. With snacks, homework, and classes, there were set goals to accomplish each day. Play time on the other hand, well as we say, not so much.

I don't have any children myself, nor do I have younger siblings or younger close cousins that I grew up with. My only real contact with youth was teaching, which again, has order and goals. For the first day of play time for the kids, I simply said they could make use of whatever was on the main floor and padded, which was most everything. I gave the kids thirty minutes to do whatever they wanted, within reason, as I watched like a hawk wondering what they were going to do. There were no set rules, only basic guidelines of "be safe and have fun."

For about a month, it went quite well. Exceedingly well, actually. I eventually started reading a book while sitting near the floor, only occasionally looking up. No issues. No injuries. No fighting. Just kids having fun. Then one day one of the students yelled out, "Ouch!" I looked up and saw him holding his eye and mildly upset. He and the other students were playing around with the padded weapons and he accidentally got hit in the eye. Nothing major, but I didn't like it and didn't want it to happen again. Because of this, I made the first rule of play time, "No hits to the face." If someone hit the face, they sat out of play time the rest of the day as punishment.

Within minutes I heard another child scream out, "Jimmy! Stop that! The rule is no hitting to the face! I hate you!" This was followed by the child running to me (clearly not injured in any way) telling on Jimmy and that he had hit her in the face. Jimmy, naturally, quickly refuted this incident by stating that he hit her on the side of the head, not the face. I now had to adjust my first rule to include no hitting to the entire head, not just the face. Problem solved, right?

The next day, I heard two students arguing yet again. "Stop hitting me in the head, Jimmy!" "I didn't hit you in the head, I hit your neck!" quipped Jimmy. And thus, my rule morphed yet again to, "anything above the shoulders." This was quickly followed by a biology lesson of what the collar bone is and whether or not it is considered part of the neck. For about two years I kept this rule of "No hitting above the shoulders" or you'll sit out of play time along with introducing numerous other rules and punishments for breaking such rules. A lot of students missed a lot of play time to say the least.

This was frustrating as I spent all of my time watching like a hawk again and replaying security cameras to determine if a child's claim of being hit in the head was real or if they were trying to get the other child in trouble. It was fifty, fifty. I finally got tired of this and changed the rule yet again. This time I told the students to please not hit the head as you risk hitting an eye (but mentioned no punishment if it happened), and simply stated, "Do whatever you want within reason during play time but be safe and if I or another staff member has to get involved, play time is over for the day." When asked what would happen if someone got hit in the head, I simply stated, "It could lead to an injury, so don't do it."

I don't recall the last time I had someone complain or get injured from being hit in the head as its quite rare that an injury occurs from it. Plus, students go out of their way to talk things out and apologize if someone does something wrong or makes a mistake as they all know if they come crying to me or a staff member, it all gets shut down no matter who's to blame.

What have we learned from this? Jimmy is a little punk. Wait, no, well, yeah, but that's not the point. The point is, issues really never came up until I introduced rules. Before I set any rules to play time, it was bliss. There was only one accidental injury in which the kid took thirty seconds to recover from and was right back in, and little to no arguing. As soon as the rules were implemented, suddenly students got into trouble for breaking the rule, which were almost always accidents, and they manipulated the rules to get others in trouble.

Despite all of the rules I set, the amount of injuries didn't go down. The complaints of injuries actually went up. Nearly every day there was a kid crying to me only to wipe away the tears and be fine seconds later. They seemed to be more upset that they perceived someone was breaking the rules rather than actually being injured. What did all of these rules accomplish? More arguments, more students punished, more frustration, the same amount of mild injuries, and extra headaches for me with less time to read my books! Why do we have hardline rules again?

I'm going to sound like an anarchist here, but rules are one of mankind's worst inventions of all time. Think about it. There is always an exception to the rule, no matter what the rule. To define the rule specifically takes a ridiculous amount of time in order to attempt to make sure the rules aren't manipulated and are as fair as possible. Look no further than our tax system, rules and loopholes everywhere.

Suggesting that we all are the same and should do the same thing, no matter who we are or what our situation is faulty reasoning. We are not the same and the situation changes everything. Hardline rules and laws remove free thinking, reasoning, logical thought and create anger. It also encourages a feeling of unfairness if we think someone is breaking the rules while we strictly follow them. When rules are set, people mindlessly follow them without thought with the assumption they are doing what's right. This is horrifying. Without these rules, we are forced to think for ourselves and decide what's best for the situation following only general guidelines, such as "Don't intentionally harm others, or "Don't be a jerk." Or, what I tell my students on a regular basis, reciting the Golden Rule of, "Do unto others as you would have done unto you."

Another example of this comes from a personal experience with my part time work at a local gym. I worked as a trainer at this gym for over a decade. My job consisted of simply being a good trainer. That was about it. I wasn't expected to be a great salesman, cleaner, booth operator, or do telemarketing. Thankfully, we had others skilled at each of those tasks. The gym was sold about ten years into my time there to another company. This new company implemented a hardline policy in which the trainers were also the sales team, customer service reps, booth operators, and birthday phone callers. We were also forced to participate in numerous meetings involving sales tactics. Virtually nothing was geared towards being a better trainer. All of this took away from time with my current clients as well as my studying efforts for future training certifications.

I was told at one point to not take, "No" for an answer and that you can squeeze out something from everyone. I had to put my foot down on this one. If you'll recall Chapter 29, #Metoobruté, then you understand my moral responsibility to accept the word "No." However, I was told that all trainers need to do this and if I couldn't do it, then I should look for another job. I still refused to follow these policies, so I was let go. The gym lost their most experienced and most educated trainer and my clients lost their trainer.

For most of my clients, I had trained them for numerous years. This hardline policy hurt the training department, the clients, the gym, and myself. All for what? A hardline policy, a rule. A rule that was written up by someone who was not involved on the front lines. This wasn't the decision of anyone at the gym, and everyone directly involved hated it. But it was a rule. And since rules have no wiggle room, everyone involved was hurt. Change this rule to a guideline or a suggestion, and things suddenly change. Understand why the policy was written rather than blindly following it, and suddenly there's a different outcome. These policies in some cases are great for the company, trainer, and client. In other situations, they are horrendous. I could go on and on with further examples and explanations, but I want to get to how this relates to martial arts and self-defense.

How do I defend against a punch? Which way do I step when being grabbed here? What do I do in this situation? These are common self-defense questions I get in nearly every self-defense seminar or class. I welcome these questions, however, there is no direct answer that covers every situation. There is no one shoe fits all rule to follow. "How do you defend against a punch?" It may seem like one or two answers will suffice, but there are numerous factors to look at.

Is the punch a jab? A cross? A lunge? A straight punch, uppercut or hook? Does the attacker have a weapon in the other hand or positioned somewhere noticeable? Do you have a weapon? Are there multiple attackers or just one? Every single one of these variables could potentially change the defense used. So one set rule cannot be applied.

When it comes to self-defense, there are no rules. I make this very clear when teaching class as I no longer teach sport martial arts. Sports have rules, self-defense does not. Students should learn ideas and understand their strengths and weaknesses. There are no specific defenses to remember for every single possibility we as instructors can think of. The situation changes constantly and so must the defenses. Students constantly place themselves and their techniques into boxes filled with rules.

For instance, when a Hapkido student is trying to learn a joint lock, a common issue that arises is that they can't get it to work properly or well enough to work on certain students. The student may ask, "If he resists, I can't seem to get to the joint lock from this grab, what am I doing wrong?" I'll ask them to show me what technique they are attempting to perform, and it almost always involves grabbing, torqueing, and over-exertion of strength.

Most students seem to forget that there is no rule that says you can't just jab your thumb into someone's eye or slap them in the family jewels to overcome strength issues. Eventually, the students hear me recite the same few responses to their answers, "It's all situational. If you're struggling to overcome their resistance, just hit them, they'll loosen up." Since Hapkido is considered a grappling art where the focus is on grabbing and joint locks, the thought of punching or kicking quickly gets forgotten and placed into a rule of, "You can't hit." To me, that's simply a bad rule.

A timely-placed solid punch, poke, or kick to a vital area can quickly overcome strength and resistance issues when you haven't perfected the joint lock. It's not easy to remove these boundaries and rules when it comes to martial arts. Plus, it doesn't help that many instructors demand these rules continue to be followed. It's understandable, however, I just don't follow it.

Historically, there may be a reason for these rules. Many martial arts styles follow set philosophy or patterns or ideas to mold their martial arts style. This can make it easier to teach and learn since all one has to do is search within the imaginary box that was created to discover the correct defense. For instance, traditional Hapkido follows three major philosophies for its techniques: circular motion, flow like water, and non-resistance. These are great guidelines to use, but in my opinion, they are just that, guidelines, not rules.

I teach many techniques in Hapkido that don't follow those guidelines. I do so because my largest focus is teaching self-defense, not teaching a style. I'll look past tradition and style rules and introduce a new technique if I feel it's useful. You can still have these guidelines to follow, without the hardline rules that most want to attach to it. After teaching students a new technique, I usually tell them to "play" with the technique. I encourage them to discover what works and what doesn't. They're urged to follow the general guidelines, but fill in the gaps with what works best for them and their body type, and their opponent's body type. I then watch carefully and make little adjustments to refine their technique.

This method also allows the student to discover why certain movements don't work. It's easy for me to tell them not to turn left and only turn right, but until they try it, they'll never fully understand why. I want them to fail on occasion to help them better understand the proper way to do things. Again, this may change depending on circumstances. This is also where sparring helps considerably. This promotes creativity and thought during class rather than mentally shutting down and blindly doing what I tell them to. That's fine if every circumstance is perfect and they never make mistakes, but that has never happened in the history of self-defense. In realistic situations, self-defense is ugly.

About ten years ago I made a dramatic change to my Hapkido program to reflect these ideas and lack of hardline rules. Hapkido is well known for having thousands of techniques to learn and memorize to cover defenses from every situation possible. The list is long and ranges from joint locks, throws and ground defenses to kicks, strikes and weapons just to name a few. There's no possible way to memorize it all and perfect it all. I consistently saw students focused just as much on armpit grab defenses that were a little "iffy" as they were on a bear hug defense (which is much more likely) that was very direct and useful. That frustrated me. Who gets grabbed in the armpit? It's possible, though, so we covered it.

I didn't like the results I was getting with students due to this process. I hesitated on changing anything as it would go against tradition and against what I thought were the "rules" of the style. I also worried that my instructor and others above me in the Federation, a group of like-minded schools working together, would shoot it down. However, one major reason our Federation was developed is to allow schools and their owners to do what they saw fit for their students and not have to be forced to do what everyone else is doing. With that in mind and encouragement from students who liked my ideas, I dramatically altered the Hapkido program I was teaching.

With this new program, I didn't feel comfortable simply calling it, Hapkido anymore, so the name, Moo Hahn Hahn Hapkido was born. Translated from Korean, this means, "Unbound Hapkido" or "Boundless Hapkido." This is a great reflection of my willingness to let go of the conventional rules and boundaries we place on our martial arts styles and life. I try and relate this unbound philosophy to my students. It's not easy, and I know there is frustration early on when I have the same responses to students' "What if?" questions with, "It depends." Eventually, they start to learn to remove restrictions in their training and expand their minds and creativity.

The next time you are stopped at a stop sign when there is obviously no other traffic around ask yourself, did I need this rule of stopping at a stop sign? Would I be less safe if it wasn't here? Would I really just blast through intersections without stopping or even looking for oncoming traffic? What may really upset you is the realization that if we suddenly took that sign down, we would blast through it, even with oncoming traffic. The invention of a stop sign removed our thought process and we simply assume that if there is no stop sign, then we have the right of way. Whereas, if there was no stop sign to begin with, we would be cautious at every intersection, because we would be more mindful of what's going on around us. Let that sink in.

.

CHAPTER 33

A sorry state of mind

Jen Van Kirk (left) training with Munazza Abraham (right). Photo by Erik Van Kirk.

From across the dojang floor I hear, "Ouch" followed by "Oh, sorry." Then a few seconds later, I hear "Ouch" followed by "Sorry." This ongoing verbalization of pain followed by an apology draws my attention. I'm now watching the culprits in question. One student applies a joint lock from their rank material they are practicing, the other student audibly winces in pain. The inflictor of the joint lock quickly apologizes as the student pops back up in order to do it again, gaining repetition.

I stare in a state of confusion with my head tilted slightly to the side like a curious puppy. Throughout class, even with different training partners, this "wince" followed by an apology continues. This must be stopped.

"Why are you saying, I'm sorry all the time?" I asked.

"Oh, I'm sorry, I didn't realize I was doing that," the student responded.

"You just apologized for apologizing," I replied.

"Oh, I'm a....I'm not going to say it, I'll try not to. It just comes out all the time. I didn't even realize I was doing it," she answered.

"I'm sorry" is one of the most pointless statements ever uttered in history of speech, and yet, the most used. Why? Does it fix anything? Does it undo that which you are apologizing for? No. We all apologize, it's just second nature to do so when you believe something inconvenienced someone. We are human, however, we make mistakes. We shouldn't have to apologize for being human. If we did whatever we are apologizing for on purpose, then we clearly aren't sorry and should accept that and change the habit moving forward. Again, saying "Sorry" doesn't change that. It may seem like saying, "I'm sorry" is no big deal and won't negatively affect your life, but it can if uttered so many times that you don't even realize you are saying it.

Let me share with you the story of Jen, the student I was quoting at the onset of this chapter. She is not alone, however, as I've had many students over the years that apologize compulsively in class. I actually had to tell her and the other students that if I hear the words, "I'm sorry" at any of their rank testings, they won't pass. But I digress, here is Jen's story.

Jen came to me years ago, and like many students, was quite hesitant as martial arts training was well out of her comfort zone. She sat in front of a computer all day doing excellent design work. However, advancements in her career as well as advancements in class seemed to be just out of reach in her current mindset of apologizing for things she didn't do wrong.

I need my students to build confidence and a positive mindset. Jen took it to heart and worked extremely hard to make changes. Not only did she take a huge step out of her comfort zone by taking a class that teaches public speaking, but I saw her actively avert from apologizing during classes. It has been a number of years since Jen first shyly walked into my studio, but all of her hard work has paid off. Jen invited me to an event for her work where employees and their family and friends are invited. I wasn't entirely sure what the event was or why I was invited, but shortly after I arrived, I understood why.

Jen, in front of an auditorium full of people, took the stage to give a speech. Not just any speech, a speech on not saying sorry. She did great! That was not the same person on that stage that first walked into my studio a few years back. I've had numerous proud moments as a martial arts instructor, most involved physical boundaries being broken such as breaking boards, competing, or watching a student earn a black belt, but the most pride comes when a student uses martial arts as a launching point to dramatically improve their life. It's something that most non-martial artists won't fully understand, but all long time practitioners realize, martial arts is life changing and goes far beyond punching and kicking. I've seen a great change in Jen's mindset, from apologizing for breathing the air near you, to being unapologetic for her gained confidence, career promotions, and success.

It may not seem like saying, "I'm sorry" is a big issue, or may even feel like a good thing. However, it can negatively affect your life in unexpected ways. At best, it's uttered so many times that it has no effect or significance for the recipient. At worst, it can be mentally demoralizing for the apologizer. Suggesting that things are constantly your fault, when they are not, can bleed over into a lack of confidence and a negative outlook.

Sadly, as a recent student pointed out to me, saying, "I'm sorry" is mandatory in some careers such as customer service representatives. It shouldn't be, as I've always found hearing, "I'm sorry..." from a customer service rep who I've never met, to be condescending and scripted. It's not their fault as it's their job, since our culture has been conditioned to say it and demands to hear it for some stupid reason. It's essentially a scapegoat. We do something wrong, we apologize for it, but don't actually change our behavior as we feel the apology fixed everything.

Understand that the point of this chapter isn't just to suggest to people to stop saying, "I'm sorry" or to be rude and unapologetic towards others. It's about having an understanding of the meaning behind the words and actions we choose. Everything we say and do effects our mood and our lives. Know that there is a difference between being a nice person and a pushover. That line gets blurred quite often when it comes to people, such as myself, who truly want to please others. We can feel like saying no to something or not apologizing suggests we are not good people, and that just isn't the case.

There is an example I give when teaching self-defense classes in which I cover not just the physical defenses, but personal boundaries and being taken advantage of. Let's say you work in cubicle land and a fellow employee states that their child is sick and they need to take off early to be with them, but they have to get a project done. They come to you asking if you would be so kind as to finish the project for them so they can be with their sick child. What do you say?

We people-pleasers undoubtedly will say yes without hesitation. That's fine, but what do you think will happen the next time their child is sick? Or some other emergency comes up? Who do you think they will go to? A different employee, or the one that helped them out last time? So, it happens again, and again, and again. The next thing you know, you're getting scolded by your boss for getting behind on your projects, and that other employee is getting a promotion for getting all of her projects done in a timely manner, thanks to you.

While this may be an exaggerated example, I hope you get the general idea that you are being a pushover and taken advantage of for being a nice person. So, do we just say, "No! Your child is awful and deserves to be sick?"

Of course not, but what we can do is say yes and be helpful while stating a clear boundary. State to the fellow employee that you can help them this one time, and one time only, if it's a serious emergency, but not on a regular basis. You've helped them, and you've set a clear boundary for future reference that they now know they shouldn't cross, all while being pleasant. This is what I mean by choosing your words and actions carefully and understanding the effect they can have on you and others. Now, go forth, be nice, and be completely unapologetic for setting personal boundaries to build your confidence, your career, and your quality of life.

CHAPTER 34

The non-discriminatory factor

Instructors and participants at a multi-school fundraising seminar.
Photo by Mark Tomes

My first real job was when I was sixteen years old. I was a dishwasher at my least favorite local restaurant. I seem to recall being able to have a steak dinner for under ten dollars if that gives you an idea of the kind of super high class restaurant this was. The senior citizens who, I assume lost their taste buds in the war, loved it though. My dad was against me working while in high school as he felt it would negatively affect my grades since the hours could be brutally long and late.

I brilliantly counterpointed his argument by explaining that I was already bombing my classes so I couldn't fall off the floor. After a verbal adjustment from my father, he allowed me to take the job if I promised to improve my grades. I agreed. I learned the first day in the kitchen that it was an absolutely disgusting job. I mistakenly didn't wear gloves or a face mask as I blindly reached into one tub of dirty dishes after another spraying high powered water at them creating a cloud of pre-chewed food around my face. I've pulled dentures, retainers, ash trays full of ashes and even dirty diapers out of those tubs and spraying all of them right back into my face and up my nose. Have you ever had baby poop mixed with cigarette ashes shot back into your face?

After a brief vomiting session, I was right back at it. I worked there for about six months and had constant cold-like symptoms, a thick layer of oil across my face and neck that I could never seem to fully remove. I even developed eleven warts on my hands that had to be frozen off. I did it all for a whopping four dollars and twenty five cents an hour, the minimum wage at the time. Needless to say, I didn't like the job, I loved it! Yes, all that stuff I mentioned was terrible, big time. Yet, there were two things that made it all worthwhile.

First, I never had money before, aside from a few dollars here and there I collected from babysitting neighbors, mowing yards, and searching friends' couch cushions to save up for a new (many times used) album from the music store across town.

Second, I loved the people I worked with. The town and state I grew up in were extremely conservative and religious. That's all I really knew. Everyone and everything I knew were homogeneous. Income level, religious and political views, cultural expectations, morals, values were all basically the same. That wasn't the case at this restaurant. Every aspect of humanity was represented in this kitchen. You name it, we had that person working in the kitchen, and then throw in a guy with breast implants who calls himself Jane.

The restaurant usually closed by ten o'clock at night, but we stayed in the kitchen cleaning and hanging out until two o'clock in the morning some days, chatting it up. I was quite hesitant of everyone the first couple of days as they were so different from anything I knew. Being around people that I didn't even know existed, let alone was ever exposed to, was extremely eye opening to me. It didn't necessarily instantly change my mind on anything, but it did open my mind to what others deal with and how all walks of life can work together and be friends even when you may be completely different. The job was so fast paced that there just wasn't time to stop and hate anyone or avoid anyone. We had to work together or the kitchen would fall apart, as the restaurant was extremely busy at all hours. None of the other jobs, classes, groups and programs I've been involved with since had this much diversity and a necessity to work together without thought, except for one, martial arts.

Walk down the street, into a restaurant, in a bar, any place, anywhere and you may see a group of people with nice shoes and clothes, others with less than formal wear, and some with a specific style of clothing or hairdo. Typically, they're in all separate groups. The formal wear talking to formal wear, the informal wear talking to the informal wear. Rich talking to rich, poor talking to poor, athletes talking to athletes, so on and so forth. Whether or not people stick to these groups because they have negative thoughts towards others or because they have more in common with the groups they're in is irrelevant. It separates us, holds us back from understanding other points of view, and solidifies how our group is the best group, albeit through ignorance.

Walk into a martial arts studio, however, and you'll notice everyone working and enjoying the company of others regardless of their gender, race, wealth, cultural background or even age and respecting each other without hesitation.

After more than twenty five years of martial arts training, I don't recall seeing discriminatory behavior on the training floor. I'm sure it's happened, I just haven't recognized it in my classroom or other schools I've visited. I've seen plenty of students not want to work with other students, but it usually had to do with one youth student seeing another youth student picking his nose and not wanting to be touched by him or an overly zealous student who always seems to go too hard. When it comes to race or religion, political views, income levels or whatever else, however, I just haven't seen it be an issue.

These days, especially, it seems to be a rarity. There is division everywhere you look. People hiding in their groups, fearing, hating or looking down on others just because they are in a different group. Martial arts has a way of stripping away your preconceived notions and any biases you may have. All that matters is the training and finding ways to be better than yesterday.

You don't even need to speak the same language. I've taught students who didn't know a single word of English. It doesn't matter. It doesn't matter how rich you are, you will get punched in the nose if you don't keep your guard up. It doesn't matter what religion you believe in or don't believe in; if you don't learn your material, you won't go up in rank. It doesn't matter who you voted for, if you don't follow your instructor's advice, you won't break that board. It doesn't matter how much stress I have when I approach the dojang floor. The second I set foot on those mats, the outside world disappears.

The only thing that matters is what's in front of me that will lead to making me (or my students) better.

I was thirteen when I took my first steps on my instructor's dojang floor. That same day a man most likely three times my age did the same thing. I knew his name and that was all. We trained together for about a year and depended on each other to improve. He was my best friend in class. We joked all class long while learning our forms and punching each other. It was great. I never would have met him if it wasn't for martial arts.

I can't count the amount of times I've had students walk into my studio as loners or outsiders who struggle to make friends, instantly make a room full of friends. A couple of years into my training, I watched as a school bully walked through the doors to sign up for classes. He had caused me a problem or two in the past, and definitely caused my friends some issues on a regular basis. He was your run of the mill, oversized, and intellectually stunted bully with an ego problem. I couldn't just ignore him, nor did the thought even cross my mind. I had to help him learn his material. I worked with him for a few minutes, and any issues we had were eliminated. He was still a jerk at school, but a jerk that would smile and say hello as we passed in the hall. Martial arts levels the playing field in a way I've never seen before and I love it.

I find myself wondering why all biases and prejudices seem to dissolve in the dojang. Could it be that we all wear the same bland uniform to disguise our economic or traditional garb? Is it that we are all there for the same reason, on the same level, respecting and learning from the same person and training in the same way with no deviation to cause arguments that lead to division? Is it that we are so focused on accomplishing a task and in need of others in class to help us accomplish that task that we don't have time to discriminate? Or is it that we just have created a bigger group to be a part of? Personally, I believe it's because the instructor is just so incredibly charming and good looking that everyone is mesmerized. I can only speak about my own school in this regard, of course, as some of my instructor friends have clearly blocked too many punches with their faces, no offense! Seriously though, I don't know. I'm just glad it does.

To be fair, martial arts isn't perfect. While I've never had issues with discrimination within class, there is still discrimination between schools or styles, unfortunately. I assume being a martial arts practitioner, there might be a bias against those who are not. However, this is on such a small scale. My point of the discrimination not being on the dojang floor and befriending those with whom you may never have met otherwise, still applies.

Thanks to martial arts, I've met nearly every different type of human on this awkward planet and befriended every one. In this day in age, where the world seems to be divided and splintered, we need martial arts more than ever. I've learned so much about people I never would have taken the time to meet elsewhere, and accepted so much about people that I may never have accepted or taken the time to learn or understand.

Maybe the answer to all of the world's problems is to train martial arts together. It certainly can't hurt. I've seen no faster way to make friends than to trade punches with them. Nothing else seems to be working, so why not give it a try?

CHAPTER 35

It's easy to do, but easier not to

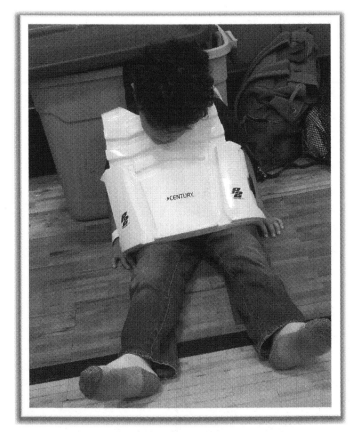

Julian Hernandez falling asleep at a tournament while waiting for his brother to compete. Photo by Dan Bourelle

"I broke my finger the other day, I can't go to the football game tonight."

"My legs are a little stiff from working in the yard yesterday, I better not go to the concert tonight."

"I have a bit of a headache, it's best I not attend the New Year's party."

All three sentences have never been uttered by anyone in the history of time. If, however, you replace the words "football game," "concert," and "New Year's Party" with the word "gym" or "dojang," then you have a sentence that gets repeated to me on a weekly basis. Why is that? How come we can magically be healed or suddenly have the strength of Superman to dismiss pain in some instances, yet have the toughness of a thin pane of glass in other instances?

I've read articles stating that laziness is natural or instinctual. Experts claim that since it takes action to do something, then it can't be natural. We don't have to take action to breathe or go to the bathroom and those are considered natural. Getting up and doing something takes action, therefore it isn't natural. I've also read articles that have stated being a hard worker is natural or instinctual. They claim that it's an evolutionary necessity to be a hard-working individual, without it, we would have not survived.

While I tend to lean heavily towards the second article, the fact remains that many, if not all of us, tend to be lazy. I know I'm not immune to being lazy. There have been countless times where my alarm chimed alerting me to get up and go to the gym and I've just laid there thinking to myself, "I am far too tired and far too comfortable to move from this spot today." And then I promptly hit the snooze button.

Is going to class that painful and excruciatingly hard? Nope, it's actually quite easy and fun once you get there. The problem is, it's even easier not to go. And therein lies the problem. How do we overcome this dilemma? Our good friend, Sir Isaac Newton has the answer.

Sir Isaac Newton's First Law of Motion states,

An object at rest will remain at rest unless acted on by an unbalanced force. An object in motion continues in motion with the same speed and in the same direction unless acted upon by an unbalanced force.

Essentially this means, a body at rest, stays at rest. A body in motion, stays in motion. The answer is creating an initial motion or action. Life keeps getting more and more convenient and less and less physical action is required. Therefore the necessity to be physically active is much higher, yet the immediate need to move is much lower.

Let's change that. Here's what works for me. I attempt to set up a training session every morning at the gym to train a client. This way, I have to get up and go to the gym, my job, my client and my reputation depends on it. If I don't have a client that morning, there's no immediate incentive to go or punishment for not going.

For yourself, try setting appointments right before you would like to go to class, that way you're already in motion getting things done, so going to the gym is now easier. Another thing that works for a lot of people is to get a gym buddy or training partner. Find a friend to train with and set a time for both of you to be there. You're much more likely to go when someone is depending on you to be there, not to mention it is much more fun. Anything that sets you in motion or creates an immediate incentive or punishment will up your chances of going to class.

My last bit of advice, don't stop, not even to take a couple of weeks for a break. Remember, a rolling stone gathers no moss! The number one cause of my clients or students quitting is due to a break. I typically see a quarter of my students leave for Christmas break each year and not return. I see clients that go on vacation and completely disregard their fitness regimen and never return. Or if they do return, they've set themselves back months. Then just as they are getting back to where they were, they go on another break and are set back again, never to proceed. They are doomed to repeat the same material over and over. Then, of course, since they don't see the progress, they give up. It's a vicious cycle.

Every time I hear a student tell me that they are going to take a short break to get things done or reset their brain or whatever excuse they tell themselves, I cringe and know I'll never see them again. I usually let them know it's a horrible idea and that it's exceedingly rare that students come back after taking a break, but there is only so much I can say or do if they've already made up their mind.

What people don't understand is that when you change your schedule and remove something like class, you will fill it with something else. And it's rare that you will fill it with something that will challenge you and be difficult. Usually it's filled with a night out with friends, or playing video games. This is why it becomes so hard to return. To come back to class means changing your schedule from something easy to do, to something hard to do. It doesn't matter how much better it is to take a class and how much fun you have once you're there or how great you feel afterward, the body only tends to recognize the right here, right now. And right now, you feel good playing the latest video game.

Don't let that broken toe nail, the minor headache, or sprained wrist keep you from improving the quality of your life with martial arts training! However, do note that there is a difference between pushing through the pain and ignoring pain. If you have a sprained knee, don't just slap on the IcyHot® and continue kicking the heavy bag. Instead, focus the training in a different area that isn't injured.

I find it important to reiterate what I've stated in Chapter 35, do not to go to the gym while sick. It should be obvious, but I see it constantly, people sneezing, coughing, wiping snot on equipment and people, yuck. You'll only be getting others sick and you won't be improving much as your body is too focused on fighting off the infection/virus.

Ultimately, find ways to keep moving and never stop. Your first year of training is a crucial year. If you can make it through one year being extremely consistent, then you have a considerably higher success rate in your training. That year will condition you, your schedule, and family/friends to adjust to your training schedule. Just don't stop.

PART III:

Observations of the Spirit

CHAPTER 36

Test, test, this is NOT only a test!

Group photo of some of Dan's students after hosting his first tournament. Back row, standing: Jen Van Kirk, Jared Kerr, Antje Almeida, Alexandra Lipford, Dan, Conor Kerr. Front row (kneeling): Ryan Estes, Enmanual Tejada, Munazza Abraham, Paulo Almeida.

Our school holds formal rank testing every three months for those who feel they are ready to progress to the next belt rank. Many schools no longer do these testings nowadays and I fully support them and completely understand why they have stopped doing them. However, I will continue to hold testings and urge my students to attend tournaments whenever possible, both for the same reason. Rank testings are far more important than just moving up in rank. In all honesty, when it comes to my lower ranks, I know who will go up in rank before the testing is even held. For higher ranks, it's a different story.

It's easy to perform your techniques in a comfortable class of people whom you know and trust, as well as, given multiple chances to do that technique just right after being properly warmed up and ready. It's not easy to perform these same techniques, however, if you are alone in front of a room full of students, family, friends and random people whom you don't know. Plus, you have to do it right the first time. This becomes incredibly difficult.

Think about it. You stand there alone, in front of a room full of strangers. The judge or judging panel has critical eyes staring at you. Your nerves start to take over, you begin to sweat. You get a little shaky and clumsy as your heart rate skyrockets through the roof and your brain suddenly takes a vacation. Why is your body not working like it does in class? Why can you not think straight to remember your next move? Why is your opponent punching and kicking your face repeatedly while you just stand there? Why does this seem exactly like something that would happen in the street if you were attacked? Because this is exactly what happens in the street when you're attacked and you have never experienced the real thing!

This is the real reason why we hold testing. This is why I push my students to enter tournaments, even when they don't feel fully ready. The knowledge you gain from this experience is crucial. Chemical changes that happen in the body when you are attacked in the street cause your brain to disappear and your limbs to suddenly move as if you're borrowing a clumsy person's body. Similar chemical changes occur when students are placed in an uncomfortable situation such as testings and tournaments.

The more you participate in these events, the better your body becomes accustomed to what your body is reacting to. Experience will help you from entering into negative reactions, or at least help you to continue your techniques if you do enter these stages. Some people thrive on these moments, others take years to overcome them. This is why we still hold rank testings. For my higher ranks, they must be able to perform properly while under these conditions in order to pass their testings.

My advice to all of those who are testing in the near future or entering a tournament is this:

Learn from it. Until the day you are forced to use these techniques to defend yourself, which I hope is never, all other situations are training situations to learn from. The only thing on the line is your time and the calories burned doing it.

Don't get too stretched out. Do a light warm up and run through your material before the testing starts. Long stretches can slow your movement and lead to injury. This is from the man who tore his hamstring stretching too much before a tournament.

Breathe. Take a moment to concentrate on your breathing, calm yourself the best you can before you begin. It will settle the heart rate and give you back control of your body.

Block out the people watching. Feel free to let their cheers boost you, but don't get distracted. Most spectators have no clue about what you are doing and will be impressed no matter how much you think you screwed up.

Own your mistakes. Don't give up or show that you made a mistake. Make it seem like you did it on purpose. It only becomes a mistake when you stop and cuss under your breath!

Take pride. When the testing or tournament is over, feel the pride overcome you knowing that so few others have just done what you did. You are awesome!

I'd like to finish this chapter with a story about my first testing. Some of my students have heard this, as well as, other "learn from my experience" stories from my past. The testing was to have a judge's panel (I believe four to six high ranking black belts) including the president of our association at the time whom I had never met. All week long leading up to the testing I kept hearing horror stories and what not to do around the president. Don't speak to him unless he speaks to you first, and be brief! Don't upset him! Don't look him in the eyes, you'll turn to stone! You know, the normal freak out stories, that turn out to be true. I'm partially joking.

He was/is a very strict martial artist, but also cared deeply about the students and eventually created a huge impact on my martial arts career. At the studio there were two large planted pots on the floor near the front of the room that had just been watered. Just before testing started they were moved to clear room for us students to be seated until we were called up to test. After we lined up and warmed up, we were commanded to move to the edge of the room and have a seat, waiting to be called up to test one at a time.

Being the overwhelmingly lucky person that I am, I had chosen to sit down where the freshly watered plants once were. The carpet was drenched in muddy water. And of course, I was wearing a thin white uniform called a dobok. I stayed put, hoping and praying that the water dried up before I was called to test. The moment had come, I was called up. I wasn't sure if anyone would notice. With the audience behind me, I stood up, yelled, "Yes Sir!" and bowed before running out onto the floor. The second I bowed, the audience busted out laughing as they saw a dirty wet water stain on my butt! I still don't know to this day how many people thought I peed and crapped myself and how many knew I had sat in water, but it was embarrassing either way!

I ran through my Taekwondo form. Then the judges, of course, asked to see the form one more time to prolong the agony. I finished my testing by going through my one-step sparring situations before finally sitting back down, with ego bruised. Embarrassing, right? But here's the important part;

that was the most pride I had ever felt in my life. I felt that I had nailed my material. That stain on my butt meant nothing! I, a fourteen-year-old introvert who was terrified to stand in front of a group, had just scoffed at my embarrassment in order to do what was needed to be done. The feeling was invigorating. This was the first step of many that led me to my passion!

That first step is a big one. It's daunting, its nerve racking, it's scary as hell, but it's also a moment that could potentially change your life forever!

CHAPTER 37

The passion of the sabumnim

Master Brent Holland (left), Joe Berry (middle) and Dan (right) between teaching sessions at a seminar. Photo by Mark Tomes

I was lucky to find my passion early in life. Many people I've met, sadly, have never found their passion. Martial arts kept me out of a lot of trouble over the years, gave me guidance, gave me goals and taught this massive introvert how to be an extrovert when needed, or at least act like one. I've watched close friends make poor choices. Some dropped out of high school or college. Others fell into heavy drug or alcohol use. I've even watched some make choices that have led to death, all due to a lack of passion to find that thing we call fulfillment.

While I love martial arts, the striking of the bag, the throwing of a man twice my size, the slight movement or touch that creates excruciating pain in the opponent, the fire that burns in the gut while competing or performing in front of hundreds or even thousands of people cheering; it's not my passion. You heard right, the martial arts are not my passion.

Did I start up my school to make loads of money? No, and my bank account can attest to that! Was it to be popular? No, my small list of friends and lack of dates and relationships over the years will tell otherwise. Was it because I have no other skills? Once again, no. I have a degree in Architectural Drafting and was quite good at my previous job. So why did I do it?

Dan with some of his youth students that had competed at their first tournament. From left to right: Jakob Strickland, Jose Hernandez, Eleanor Ward, and Andrew Arabian.

While family, friends, and students may be confused by this, my fellow instructors will hopefully understand. I love martial arts deeply, but my passion is helping others discover what martial arts can offer. What moves me is the look in someone's eyes when they realize strength and power have nothing to do with how big your muscles are. The mile-wide smile on a student's face when that seemingly impossible technique finally "clicks" and is done flawlessly. Seeing that look of confidence on a student's face who spent his childhood being bullied and a victim due to low self-esteem. Seeing the adult student who gets out of her car with the weight of the world on her shoulders and stress so high the steam seeps out her ears and eyes, completely alter her disposition once she steps onto the training floor. Seeing so many lives transform is my passion. When I see true focus, concentration, and a sense of control over one's body and life, I know I've made a difference.

Photo taken of Dan (left) with Master Tony Morris (middle) and Master Mark Nathanson (right) during his visit to Asheville Sun Soo Martial Arts School.

Creating all of those situations and possibilities, and blogging about them has given me hope. By compiling my posts into this book, I hope to reach even more people, and those who I can't physically help in my studio. My passion is not physically hurting people, though inflicting harmless pain from time to time can be quite fun. I've already been down that road and it doesn't fill any holes in my heart or give me a sense of accomplishment. Helping others does. When my efforts have failed me, when friendships or relationships have hurt me, when life has let me down, martial arts, teaching, my passion, has always lifted me back up, no matter how hard I was knocked down.

I began teaching classes when I was about seventeen-years-old, shortly after receiving my first black belt in Hapkido. Like most teenagers, I felt ignored, talked down to, underestimated, and thought the worst of by society. I had a lot to say, a lot of questions that I wasn't allowed to ask, and just wanted some recognition for my efforts. The Hapkido class I trained in and eventually taught, was primarily law enforcement and adult males between the ages of twenty and sixty five. In all aspects of life, that age group would never put much effort or trust in me, except in the dojang. When teaching that class, I was respected, looked up to, and someone others sought answers from. It boosted my confidence and gave me a very clear path in life for the first time ever.

Instructors who taught at our first multi-school fundraising seminar. From left to right: Master Burnie Richardson, Dan, Master Brent Holland, Master Jim Irwin, Master Jeffrey Rohena, Travis Moore. Photo by Mark Tomes

Occasionally, we would have a new student try out a class and see me, a scraggly pimple faced teenager, teaching classes and scoff at the idea of me guiding them or knowing anything that would help them learn self-defense or obtain whatever their goals were. However, I consistently won them over by the end of class. If need be, I would spar them if I felt they were slipping away and that would correct and humble them. Have you ever seen a two hundred pound, former collegiate athlete, aggressive male be "humbled" by a one hundred twenty five pound, seventeen-year-old with zits and goofy hair? It's glorious! These are the things that showed me my path, what my true passion was and what I wanted to do the rest of my life.

Why do I write this? To boost my ego and let everyone know I'm a better instructor than others? No, and I am not. I write this for two reasons. First, to help others try and discover their own passion in life, their purpose, their own personal answer to the question, "Why am I on this earth?" Second, like many of my writings, I want to break the stereotype that martial arts are all about a bunch of brutes who like to fight. It's an ongoing battle, but it's a battle I will fight to win until I die.

Fighting is just a tool that is used to build character, responsibility, discipline, inner strength, health, or as listed in the previous paragraph, a way to humble people into learning from someone they didn't expect to learn from. I could go on and on about the benefits but you get the idea. Martial arts steered me away from bad choices and led me to my passion for helping others. I know it has this same affect for everyone who takes this life long journey in martial arts.

CHAPTER 38

Why?

"The Championship match is about to begin!"

"First competitor to five points wins!"

"Judges ready?"

"Yes Sir!" is shouted out in unison from opposite sides of the ring.

"Fighters ready?" A loud intimidating yell bursts out from each of the competitors and fills the arena.

"BEGIN!"

I've seen this guy before. He's good. He's real good. Undefeated. And tall. I hate tall competitors! I'm not sure if I can beat him.

The crowd, they're cheering loudly. His crowd is cheering louder than mine. Do I have a crowd? Is anyone rooting for me?

My back is sore. So is my neck. Took a hard hit in my last match, a headache is settling in. My hamstring is still sore and tight from being torn a few months back. I wish I was feeling better. Enough thinking, time to start moving.

We're feeling each other out. Finding our distances. I'm going to take a chance. Incoming flurry!

Two competitors sparring at the annual Warrior Cup tournament that Dan's studio hosts. Photo by Jen Van Kirk.

"BREAK!"

"JUDGES CALL POINT!"

Well that was a mistake, 1-0 him. Mental notes taken.

Some feints are thrown to see how the other will react. I shoot in quickly as if to attack, and then shoot back out. He throws out a front leg kick to defend.

I now know his natural reaction, next point will be mine!

I jump in once more knowing he will throw that same defensive kick in an attempt to keep me away. I roll out and block the kick as I pivot on my front foot and spin one hundred eighty degrees to my back looking over my shoulder to find my opening. It may seem like a split second, but it's all the time I need to find an opening and counter with a kick of my own. My heel drives deep into his abdomen.

Is that his spine I felt through his stomach?

He keels over at the loss of breath and pain. I hear a mix of groans from those in the crowd who feel his pain and cheers from those who were impressed with the counter.

Two more competitors sparring at the Warrior Cup fundraising tournament. Photo by Jen Van Kirk.

"BREAK!"

"JUDGES CALL POINT!"

I knew the next point was mine! 1-1 tie.

He's got his breath back, and doesn't look happy. He just switched to the next gear.

He bursts off the line from the start and explodes into a flurry.

I don't think he cares about a point here, he wants to prove something.

A scuffle of hard hits are exchanged.

"BREAK!"

There were multiple points scored here, which way did the judges see it?

"JUDGES CALL POINT!"

No! They gave it to him. 2-1 him. I caught a hard strike to the nose in that scuffle. I think it's bleeding. I don't know for sure though as I refuse to address it. Can't make it look like I was affected by it.

He sees me trying hard not to want to wipe my nose. He knows I was affected by it.

I can see his confidence rising. He's going to try something big, I know it.

The next flurry ensues. An amazing display of technique is flowing back and forth. Lightning fast kicks stretching their limits, turns, jumps, blocks, counters, counters to counters. It's all coming out. A break in the action to regroup before the next flurry as no points are called.

Did I just tear my other hamstring in that last flurry? Seriously? Ugh. Keep moving, don't let it tighten up. The sweat is dripping quite profusely from my forehead, around my eyes, down my cheek, rolling down to the tip of my jaw before it pours to the ground. May need to get out my floaties to finish this match.

He suddenly slides in at a strange angle.

I don't recognize this movement.

As I stand, staring in amazement of what I'm seeing, he flips onto his hands as if to do a cartwheel. A foot or two, possibly three, strike my head.

"BREAK!"

"JUDGES CALL POINT!"

What was that?! Did he just break-dance kick me and score a point?! Yet another mental note taken. He's up 4-1. Head kicks are two points in this tournament, even when you're standing on your hands.

He's not the only one with tricks up his sleeve.

His hands are getting lower from too much confidence, or fatigued from standing on this hands. Get your cameras out, it's my turn.

I subtly slide back before launching into the air towards him. While in the air I load up a massive kick.

Is he floating in air? Are there cables attached somewhere? He's been up there forever!

I believe I've spotted someone in the crowd checking his watch and taking a sip of coffee while up here. I know I've been up here for too long. It's too obvious of a kick. Everyone in the arena knows a kick is coming. My competitor being one of them. That's why I suddenly pull the kick back and land a punch to the side of his head!

Two competitors in the women's division of the Warrior Cup tournament. Photo by Jen Van Kirk.

"BREAK!"

"JUDGES CALL POINT!"

Fooled you! I'm starting to sneak back! He's still up though 4-2.

I slide in with a deceptive hook kick. It shoots out behind him, hooks back in with a direct path to the back of his head. He's too good to take that hit though, and I know it. He ducks under the kick as expected. The kick suddenly reverses direction while in air just as it passes his head and drives back in connecting with his forehead.

He wasn't expecting that, he was off balance when he ducked. He is now unwillingly sitting on the ground with the assistance of my foot to his head.

I smile.

He smiles.

I help him up.

The crowd is cheering. They clearly no longer have a favorite. They just love the action.

"BREAK!"

"JUDGES CALL POINT!"

I'm catching up, 2 points for the head kick. It's all tied up 4-4. It's sudden death. It doesn't matter though, I've already won this. I see it in his eyes, he's done all of his tricks and I'm still standing. I on the other hand, still have more surprises. I'm exhausted though; do I have enough in me? And then it hits me...

There it is. It's what I've been waiting for. It's where every athlete wants to be.

I'm in "the zone." The place where points don't matter. Where all movement is done with ease and without a thought. Where winning and losing is no longer a thought. The pain? What pain? I feel nothing. Only appreciation of every limb, every finger, every toe and the way they all move.

I don't believe I'm standing on the ground anymore. I'm just hovering, moving with ease. The crowd noise? What crowd noise? I hear nothing but what I need to hear. My breathing? I'm fairly certain I've stopped breathing through my nose and mouth and have evolved into just soaking the oxygen in through my skin.

My competitor? What competitor? I have no competition. I can't be defeated anymore. That would involve winning and losing, there is no such thing because there is no future. There is only now. There is no more "me" controlling my body. There is no more separation of body, mind, and spirit. There is only I as a whole. The fifth point is only a number, no longer an attainment.

Why do we do what we do? Why does a football player sacrifice his body to play? Why does a skater attempt to ride that rail despite falling a hundred times? Why does one jump out of an airplane for seemingly no reason. Why does a gymnast or a cheerleader sacrifice life and limb to soar through the air? Why do we do this to ourselves?

It's how we find our limits, just to learn we have no limits. It's to find that moment when we leave our physical body and survive only as one being. No longer separated or at odds with ourselves. No more mind holding back the body. No more body deflating the spirit. No more Spirit limiting the mind. It's how we go beyond surviving in this world and actually live and feel alive. This is why we do what we do.

Oh, and It's also because, "pain heals, chicks dig scars, and glory lasts forever" – *Shane Falco, The Replacements.*

CHAPTER 39

Anger

One moment can last an eternity.

I looked up the word "anger" on various online dictionaries. There are multiple, different definitions of "anger," but the one I liked the most came from Wikipedia®. It states, "Anger is an emotion related to one's psychological interpretation of having been offended, wronged, or denied and a tendency to react through retaliation."

I liked this definition the best because of one word. Interpretation. This word tells us that we can change and control this emotion by the way we perceive and interpret situations.

Everyone enters martial arts for various reasons, and there are numerous benefits, including controlling anger. But like most any skill, it must be recognized and steps must be taken to improve it or nothing will change. And like with any skill, it's an ongoing process that must be practiced regularly.

Those who know me, know that I am not quick to anger. Even close friends have never seen me angry, or even upset. Despite what some may think, this is not because I am emotionless. I think the best way to explain my attitude when it comes to anger is best told in a story. I have only told this story to two people and that was seven years after the incident occurred. I tell this story for two reasons, as a cautionary tale and as a form of therapy as I found talking about the story was extremely helpful to me.

As an avid baseball/softball player, I was highly competitive and didn't take losing well. Even when our team won, if I had a poor performance, I was still upset. It was toward the end of the 2001 softball season and we were in the playoffs. Our team was quite dominant for a number of years and winning was the norm. We fully expected to win the league championship.

During one of the playoff games one of my best friends, Andy, had come home to visit and was at the ballpark that day. I had known Andy since the fifth grade. We became friends instantly when he transferred to our school and had stayed close friends for years until life sent us in two different directions. I had only seen Andy a few times since high school, especially after he had moved to another town. So, when I saw him at the ballfield watching us play, I was excited to catch up with him and learn what he' been up to over the past couple of years.

Quickly though, my excitement turned to frustration, which turned to anger as I made one bad play after another on the field, culminating in losing the playoffs. As usual, when I played poorly or lost a game, I wanted nothing to do with anyone. I just wanted to go home and be alone. I was inconsolable. So after the game when Andy and I should have been heading out for a night on the town and to renew our friendship, I instead was too overwhelmed with anger that I walked on past him and went straight home without so much as a goodbye. I'll see him another time, I thought to myself.

A few days later, Andy decided to drive back home. During the drive back home his car went off the road and crashed. Andy died on August 1, 2001.

It wasn't the fact that I didn't get a chance to say goodbye that got to me, most don't get to say goodbye to friends and family when that day comes; it was the fact that I had the chance to say goodbye and I let anger take that from me. That same anger, as well as denial, also led me to avoid his funeral. I refused to believe that he had died. It had to be another Andy in that car accident, I told myself. To make matters worse, I blamed myself for his death for years, assuming that if I had stayed and spent time with him that day, I could have altered the outcome. Maybe he would have stayed longer, or left at a different time or even just had a different mindset to keep him on the road. Over time though, I accepted that my thinking that way wasn't going to change anything for the better.

I still to this day have a reoccurring dream in which I'm talking to Andy. The location is different every time, but the situation is always the same. He walks into the room, sits down with me and we talk. I ask his advice on things, he answers. You see, I looked up to Andy, more than any other friend I ever had. I always asked him questions. It was even Andy who told me about the birds and the bees. Hah! Quite shocking to a ten-year-old! The dreams always ended the same way. With me realizing that he had died and asking him, "But I thought you were dead?"

And he always replies, "I'm talking to you, aren't I?" He was right. Even in death he was still teaching me life lessons. You see, from that point on, whenever I have ever gotten close to being angered or losing my cool, the first thought in my head is, "Is being angry over this really worth it?" I'm instantly reminded of that event that happened years ago. I'm not saying I'm perfect, I've still had my slip ups, but I can count on one hand how many times I've lost my temper since that day, and that hand could be missing a few fingers.

My story is really no different than anyone else's. The names and dates change, situations change, but the impact is the same. The feeling of anger is normal, it's going to happen. It's how we react that's important, as it's the reaction that we can control. Over the years I've found things that have worked to control my temper. I have also searched around the internet and found some additional steps that can be taken to help control the temper. They are as follows:

Anger can, many times, come from ignorance. I see this happen quite often, a quick reaction to a small amount of information, or misinformation. Make sure your reaction to anger is warranted before you act. Like with nearly all conflicts, most situations can be dissolved through gaining more information and intelligence.

Deep breathing. As mentioned in Chapter 11, breathing exercises can help control that which we don't have direct control over. Anger is one of those things. Breathing exercises are widely known to lower blood pressure and have a calming effect on the body. Plus, focusing your attention on breathing takes your attention away from stewing in your anger!

Don't hold it in, talk it out. There's something magical about getting it all out. It just makes us feel better, even if the issue is never solved. Holding it in just causes us to stew over the issue and make it worse. Once we get it out, it tends to stay out. This also helps us control when we let out this emotion. Allowing it to come out in a proper way is quite healthy!

Use "I" instead of "you". This is an extension of the previous "talk it out" suggestion. Using "you" implies it's the other person's fault and can escalate a situation, where "I" is a bit more passive. For example: Use, "I feel frustrated when I don't receive help when I ask", as opposed to, "You never help when I ask." Keep the emphasis on how you feel, not what they did or are doing to you.

Understand the situation from all angles. Put yourself in the other person's shoes. Often times, you'll find that they acted the same way you would have acted. We all have our reasons for doing what we do and very few of us go out of our way to harm others intentionally.

Think positive. Think of an upcoming event you are looking forward to. For me, this is quite possibly the best way to avoid anger, frustration, and sadness. I work hard to set up something each and every week to look forward to. Thus, when a situation arises that upsets me, I think of that event that I've been looking forward to, and it immediately changes my attitude.

Exercise. Who here didn't think I was going to mention this one? Anyone? Anyone? Beuller? Beuller? I can throw down an entire list of things that exercise helps with when it comes to anger. From the mood enhancing hormones that are released to the feeling of accomplishment to simply keeping the mind occupied, the positives are numerous. If you haven't figured it out by now, exercise is always the answer!

Be proactive. Last but not least, don't procrastinate and wait for that life altering moment. You can change today. It seems as though this is the way most of us work, we wait for something to break before we fix it. Far too many clients come to me for fitness training after their health has become an issue. Most women don't take my women's self-defense class until after they've been a victim or have been in a scary situation. The same is true for anger management; don't wait until it has been court ordered, or when it has forever scarred you. Start the process now! One moment can forever alter your life, it's up to you to decide if it's going to be negative or positive.

CHAPTER 40

A candle in the dark

The candle Dan used during a Masters Ceremony.

Photo by Dan Bourelle

I write this chapter with a heavy heart, as my father, who had battled cancer for the past year and a half, passed away on July 16, 2013. Many of my memories as a child and even as an adult are marked by music, and this occasion was no different. Songs played in my head throughout the whole ordeal of preparing for the funeral. One of which was the song, Each Small Candle. This song was written by Roger Waters, the former bassist and creative force behind Pink Floyd, and was inspired by an act of "heart and pride" during an

Albanian/Serbian conflict in which an Albanian soldier broke ranks to tend to a Serbian civilian in need of help. The lyrics culminate in the statement, "Each small candle lights a corner of the dark."

That one act of kindness shown by the soldier helped shine a light in the darkness of war. While preparing for the funeral service, I sat down with my brothers and my aunt and uncle, and shared stories of my father. The last comment made was from my Aunt Wanda, who said, "He was like a candle in the dark." She was right. My father, as a teacher, lit the candles from his blazing flame to all of his students. Not just students either, but everyone he came in contact with throughout his entire life. This quote quickly attached the song to my father and this chapter was written.

Read magazines, social media posts, watch the news, listen to your friends and family, and you'll hear the complaints of a world gone mad and headed in a downward spiral. It's all over, you can't miss it. Everyone sees the mistakes made and are quick to point the finger, even if it's at the wrong person or incident. There is always someone to blame. The darkness is everywhere.

But for some reason, we forget two very important things. First, there is much more "good" in this world than there is "bad", despite what some may think. Second, most people never seem to want to change. We just want to point out what's wrong, and seem to have no intention of correcting it. Why? Is it because we are lazy? Is it because we don't know how to fix it? Is it because we feel it's a lost cause? I don't believe it's any of these things.

I believe it's because people truly, despite what they might say, believe that one person cannot make a difference in this world. I have only one thing to say to that. You are wrong. Normally I am a "live and let live" type of person, and feel everyone is entitled to their own opinion, but I have to put my foot down on this one and repeat myself. You are wrong if you believe that one person cannot make a difference.

One candle can light one hundred other candles, and yet never lose its own light. It takes only one person to step up and the rest will follow. By nature, most of us don't want to make decisions, we want to follow. Remember back in school when you had a question to ask, but didn't ask it because you didn't want to sound stupid since no one else was asking questions?

But then there was that one kid who raised his hand and asked the first question, and then the rest of the room suddenly had questions. That one kid was the candle that lit and inspired the rest of the room. While one person alone may not be able to fight a giant or change the world, that one person can inspire others, more than enough, to make that change.

Most of us are like sheep, we stay put and do nothing until forced to move, and we're comfortable in that spot. Our only movement is forced, whether it be a sheepdog herding us, or a wolf chasing us in a new location. We don't have to live the life of a sheep though, we can choose at any point to stand up, shed the sheep skin and create our own destiny which will inspire others. Become that candle that lights one hundred others.

As I sifted through memories and thoughts about my father's life, I couldn't help but come back to his death, more than I cared to. However, even in the darkness of his death, I found yet another candle shining brightly, more than one actually. When I arrived at Dad's home, after a long flight and a trip to the hospital, I went into the bathroom. What did I see? A rifle sitting right next to the toilet. I couldn't help but burst out laughing. "Welcome to Nebraska" I thought to myself. If I didn't know any better, I swear my dad placed this here just to get a laugh in a time of grief. I found out later that he used it to shoot rabbits from the bathroom window, and possibly wandering neighbors in the back yard. Sorry PETA® people, but that's just funny.

The pellet gun that Dan's father kept in his bathroom to shoot at rabbits through the window. Photo by Dan Bourelle

I feel it's important to note that it was a pellet gun. As the funeral date neared, I recalled a time when I was six years old. I was at my mother's funeral, in a room with my cousins away from the crowd. I don't recall all of the emotions I went through that day, but I recall one, anger. Not from my mother's passing, but from the fact that my cousins and brothers were laughing and telling jokes in this room. They weren't telling jokes about the funeral, they were remembering my mother and some of the funny moments they spent with her. But this upset me.

I couldn't understand why someone would be anything but sad at a funeral. Over the years though, I've come to understand. It too was that candle in the darkness, a break from the sadness of the situation and a celebration of an amazing woman.

This time, at my father's funeral, I embraced it as my brothers, cousins, aunts, uncles and friends lightened the mood with their amazing humor and stories that put a smile to my face. This time, I was a candle willing to be lit.

With death comes new life. More thoughts rushed through my head as I looked to the future. Through such big changes in life, vast other changes come about. They can be negative or they can be positive. The key is understanding that we ourselves have the most influence on if that change will be negative or positive. We must choose, and actively pursue this positive change. As strange as it sounds, I see many positive changes in my life from my father's death. Invigorated by mortality, knowing there is no time to waste or procrastinate. Don't get me wrong, I would exchange it all in a moment to bring him back, but since I am unable to do so, I will make a positive change from the negative situation.

As it relates to martial arts, I see this same decision making happen in the classroom when presented with an obstacle. Whether it be a difficult, seemingly impossible technique, or a board that refuses to break, or that one student that you just can't seem to get an advantage over when sparring. There are always obstacles. Sadly, most will simply quit, never to return.

As an instructor, this kills me as I feel it is on my shoulders to guide my students through these tough moments. But at the same time, I can only do so much. I can open that door of opportunity, but I can't push them through it and I must let these students go.

On the other end, I have students that push harder, relentlessly, to overcome the obstacle. It is at that time that the inner flame begins to burn bright and inspire others, including myself. In the dojang, the entire school must work to help each other overcome these obstacles as not only will the favor be returned, but that energy it creates, when they do overcome it, inspires the rest to work harder. Each student works to build that flame and, in time, light the wick of other students.

In years past, our association would hold a Master's Ceremony whenever someone reaches the rank of sixth degree black belt and earns the right to the title of Master.

During this ceremony, the lights are turned out and the highest ranking teacher sits at the front of the room with a lit candle in front of him/her. It's the only visual light seen, albeit small. From there, each student that instructor has taught, one by one, lights their candle from the head instructor's candle and proceeds to sit down in front of him/her.

Then the students from those instructors light their candles from that group who taught them, and so on and so on until every student's candle has been lit, all stemming from one initial candle. This represents perfectly what this chapter is all about. That one highest ranking instructor and his candle representing knowledge/inspiration, inspired and enlightened one hundred (or more) students. By the end of the ceremony, if there are enough students participating, the entire room will be lit as if someone turned on all of the lights.

You don't have to be super human, have a powerful job, or be rich to inspire others. Nor do you have to inspire one hundred people. You just have to inspire one to pass that flame along and brighten the day, year, or life of another. We're all capable of inspiring others; we just have to make the choice to do so. If one small candle lights a corner of the dark, imagine what a billion small candles can light.

Dan's father, brothers and Dan outside of his grandmother's home in 1989. From left to right: Mike Bourelle, Gene Bourelle, Roury Bourelle, and Dan.

CHAPTER 41

The helping of the humbled

Two of many instructors who have graciously helped Dan over the years. Master Brent Holland (left), Master Burning Richardson (middle), and Dan (right). Photo by Mark Tomes.

Many of us have New Year's resolutions. We have resolutions to get into shape, learn something new, or change something broken. Happiness starts within. The first step begins with you. Only you can change your life. We recite these statements to ourselves thinking they alone are going to be what changes us. These statements are true. We are largely in control of our own happiness and success. However, we must not forget that the greatest goals in life, or even some of the smallest ones, can't be done alone.

Life is a multi-player game, not meant to be played solo. The man who walks alone with the assumption of succeeding is a fool. I know this because I've been a fool on many occasions. I've always been a bit stubborn when it comes to asking for help. But I'm working on it. I've run my martial arts studio, and everything involved with it, on my own for many years. I wasn't just the instructor, I was the janitor, the marketing director, the sales person, the event coordinator, the secretary, and so on.

The first year I started my after-school program, I even drove the van to pick up all the kids. One day, I woke up sick. Try as I might, I couldn't get over it in time to pick up the kids, but I had to. So I grabbed a puke bucket and sat it between my legs as I drove off to get the kids. I kept saying to myself, "Please don't throw up." I did well. Until the last leg of the drive, just two blocks away, sitting at a stop light, it blew. I hurled chunks into the bucket as quietly and inconspicuously as I could as to not worry the kids.

I almost got away with it, until I heard Dillon, who was sitting right behind me, ask, "Mr. Dan, are you okay? Are you throwing up?" "I'm okay Dillon, don't worry," I replied hoping he didn't see me vomiting. "Mr. Dan is throwing up guys," he yelled to the rest of the van full of kids. I failed. I got them to the studio and got through the day and swore that wouldn't happen again.

The next day I decided to hire a driver and assistant. I couldn't afford it, but I also couldn't afford not to. What would happen if I was too sick to drive or needed to go to the hospital? Who would run the program? I can't just not pick the kids up. Parents trust that their kids are in good hands. I needed help. I've had an assistant and drivers ever since and my life is considerably easier when it comes to running the after-school program.

Whether it's someone guiding us, walking along side us, or pushing us from behind, we all need help to attain our goals. It all may begin from within, but once it hits the surface, it's a united effort. In the martial arts, each individual has their own goals and their own pace, but going at it alone is the least efficient way of training. We need instructors to teach us, fellow students to help motivate us and push us harder, and eventually students of our own to help keep us on our toes with fresh questions and ideas leading us to continue our own studies so we don't become stale.

We also must stop and ask ourselves, "What are we truly searching for?" Do you want to get in shape for a healthier you? Or is it because you want the beauty next door to recognize you? Many of us seek more money. Why? It's simply paper. Not even that anymore, now it's just numbers being sent from your employer to your bank and then to the store where you make your purchases. What do you want to come from that money? That is your true goal. This is important; as it may change your entire path to success and who you seek help from.

Whether we're in need of a guiding hand from a friend, a partner in life, a mentor, spiritual guidance, or maybe even a bunch of minions to do your bidding, we must understand that desire, courage, strength, intelligence and money may get you started on your path, but these attributes will never be enough as some things in life go beyond what we can do alone.

CHAPTER 42

Don't let Bo Jackson stifle your dreams

When I was about ten-years-old my father took me and my brothers to Kansas City to watch the Kansas City Royals® play the Baltimore Orioles®. I played baseball for as long as I could remember and had dreams of playing professionally, like most little league players. I was excited. It was my first professional baseball game, my first professional game of any sport for that matter. Not only that, but a man widely known as the greatest athlete in professional sports was going to be playing, Bo Jackson. My memory isn't the greatest, so I may be off a little on this, but I believe Bo hit fifteen home runs in one game that day, give or take a couple. I was in awe of the players. I was also crushed. Crushed because that is when I realized I had no chance of being a professional baseball player. These people were athletic gods. I was just a lowly human.

Like with any sport, hobby, or career, there are people out there that are extremely good at what they do and others that are just average. I see many students look at these talented individuals and get frustrated, suggesting that they will never be that good so they may as well quit. We tend to see the negative side of things quicker and more often than the positive. We focus on what we can't do rather than what we can do. We see those who are better than us rather than those we are better than. We also tend to forget that some people are great because they worked hard to become great. It didn't happen overnight and they very well may have been mediocre when they first started. We can't let these people stifle our dreams and aspirations just because we don't feel we can be better than they are or even equal, especially when it comes to martial arts.

As I've mentioned numerous times in previous chapters, martial arts mean different things to different people. One may be physically talented and able to defend himself easily with his physical abilities, but how is that any better than the person who is more gifted in reading people and their actions and able to avoid the physical altercation to begin with? Did they not just both defend themselves from harm? There is no set standard for greatness in the martial arts. Some are good with kicking and striking. Others are good with grappling. Some are good with weapons, and some with knowledge and cerebral abilities. Others have been successful at using martial arts as a way to become healthier.

At a tournament years ago, I watched a sparring match, one very talented individual and one with skills elsewhere, so to speak. The competitor, as well as everyone around the ring, knew he had no chance. As the referee yelled, "Begin" the competitor paused, stepped back out of his fighting stance and put his hands up as if to say, "hold on a second" and pointed behind the other competitor frantically. The other, more skilled, competitor quickly stopped and looked over his shoulder. And upon doing so, was quickly punched in the back of the head for a quick easy point. The oldest trick in the book may be old, but people still fall for it! There are no rules in the rule book about distractions. Did that competitor win? Of course not, he got pummeled five to one in points. The point is, there was no reason he should have gotten that one, yet he found a way around his lack of physical skill set to get that point.

Master Burnie Richardson (left), Master Jim Irwin (middle), and Dan (right), chatting at the end of a tournament after judging together. Photo by Mark Tomes.

It's not always about winning. The root of most gained knowledge and skills are based on self-improvement. Learning about yourself, improving yourself, catering to your strengths, protecting or removing your weaknesses, these should be your goals. If attaining those goals happens to lead you to a win in a competition or elsewhere, fantastic. Don't compare yourself to others. Who they are has nothing to do with you and who you are. If being around and watching people that are great at what you want to be great at helps inspire and drive you, that's fantastic, continue to be inspired by them. But if it just brings you down and takes the wind out of your sails, it's time to stop paying attention to them and spend more time on yourself. You're more important.

CHAPTER 43

A lesson in humility, through humiliation

It's November of 1994, I have just recently turned fourteen and am only a few weeks into my training in Taekwondo. I am still a white belt, but learning fast. I'm quite confident in my skills, albeit new skills. I had grown up playing sports and was very active and athletic. I didn't need martial arts to learn self-defense, I was already good at fighting. I'm just here to prove it, and to enjoy dominating yet another physical activity.

It's my first day of sparring. I was excited to spar for the first time! Then I saw my opponent. It was an eleven-year-old girl, and only two ranks higher than me. Maybe she was twelve. Either way, I didn't want to beat up a girl, let alone a small girl who was younger than me. I'll go easy on her, then hopefully I'll spar one of the adults and show them how great I am.

A great kick to the head, a sharp punch to the gut and a kick that was good enough to be framed and hung on a wall. If only those techniques came from me. I feel the bruises swelling, but don't want to show it. Is that blood wanting to exit my nose? Sniff it back up. Hope no one saw that. I must have gone too easy. I was trying too hard to do proper technique rather than just win. I could have won if I really wanted to. I .... I .... I was beat by a twelve-year-old girl. She might be eleven. I'm not as good as I thought I was. She was great. I want to be that great. I'm hooked on martial arts. I want to learn more!

This was a big moment early on in my martial arts journey. It was when I first learned about humility. Keep in mind that humility and humiliation are two different words with two different meanings. Humility is that of being humble while humiliation is that of being embarrassed. However, that doesn't mean one can't lead to the other. I was humiliated, embarrassed, but it led to my humility, my humbleness.

While it should be obvious as to why we need to have humility and be humble in the martial arts, and in life, it's tough to accept. Accepting that we have humility feels as though we are showing that we aren't good enough. We work incredibly hard to be good, why would we suggest that we are not?

Look at most professional fighters, do they seem humble? Overwhelmingly, no. They tend to display their confidence and arrogance on epic proportions. So, is it necessary to have humility in the martial arts? I don't know. Look at someone like Muhammad Ali, arguably one of the greatest fighters of all time. Was he humble? Maybe outside of the ring and behind closed doors, but never in front of the camera or in the ring. He was confident and cocky. He gave us the quote, "When you're as great as I am, it's hard to be humble!"

Maybe this confidence drives them to be better, knowing that around every corner there is someone wanting to humble them. One needs to keep in mind, though, that there is a big difference between sport and traditional martial arts. A sport is about winning, martial arts is a lifestyle that is meant to improve the quality of one's life. With that understanding, while it may be okay for a sport fighter to lack humility, it works against those who train in martial arts. A true martial artist knows that we are always working to be better. We are competing only with ourselves. Bad, good, great, amazing, they all mean nothing. We only work to get better. The only way to get better is to recognize we aren't perfect and this is where humility comes in.

Ultimately, it's not necessarily having or not having humility, it's a matter of recognizing it. In a way, we all have it, but many hide it or ignore it. Unfortunately, this could mean you will never grow, as you will retain your ignorance of your humility, and ignorance never creates intelligence. It's only when you recognize your shortcomings, letting go of your ego and arrogance, will you truly begin to learn.

The choice is inevitably yours. You can choose to be humble, or you can be forced into being humbled through humiliation. They both seem to work quite well.

CHAPTER 44

Violence, our misunderstood brother

Dan (white sparring gear) sparring during a multi-school fight night.
Photo by Mark Tomes.

Viciously attacking another person with no regard for their life when they haven't attacked you.

Killing another human being.

Killing a race or large group of people.

At first read, these most likely look like all horrible acts to most of you. For the rest of you, you are what are known as a psychopath or sociopath, or you know where I'm going with this chapter. Let's add context to these seemingly horrific acts of human nature.

Viciously attacking another person with no regard for their life when they haven't attacked you:

1. The person viciously attacking another is doing so because they want to steal your money or other items.
2. A parent sees her child being abducted or attacked by an adult stranger who has bad intentions.

Killing another human being:

1. A murderer killing another human being over a verbal argument.
2. A homeowner shoots and kills an armed intruder who clearly had intent to kill.

Killing a race or large group of people:

1. Committing genocide because they don't believe that race or group of people are equal or deserving of life.
2. Killing a group of people that you are at war with to secure freedom and protect your country.

All of these scenarios are considered violent. But the first scenario is considered bad while the second acceptable or necessary. Yet when society speaks of violence, it always seems to be in a negative view, as if the second scenarios in each group listed above aren't violent. I assure you, they most definitely are.

Our society tells everyone that we need to eliminate violent behavior and that all violence is evil. I know a lot of people don't want to hear this, or don't want it to be true, but to eradicate violence, is to eradicate ourselves. We are a viciously violent species and it was, and to an extent, still is, necessary. Without it our species or countries, would never have survived and flourished. It's in our nature, every one of us, to be violent. I don't care how peaceful you think you are, it resides in you.

There was a shocking experiment that was conducted back in 1971 by Philip Zimbardo named, "The Stanford Prison Experiment." Zimbardo conducted the Stanford prison study in which twenty four clinically sane volunteers were randomly assigned to be "prisoners" or "guards" in a two week mock prison scenario. This study into prison life was cut short after just six days due to violent behavior and emotional trauma. The volunteers knew they were being used in a study, but they did not know when the study was to begin or what role they would play in the scenario.

Half of the participants were suddenly arrested one morning and put into prison. The participants that were assigned as guards were allowed to do whatever they felt was necessary to maintain order in the prison. This free rein of authority quickly spiraled out of control as did the erratic behavior by the prisoners who were unfairly stripped of their freedoms. Both the guards and the prisoners were noted as exhibiting "sadistic" behavior during the experiment. The experiment was halted as emotional trauma set in and physical violence was shown to be the next step. Remember, these were proven clinically sane and average individuals that were participating.

While this study shows how even good people can do evil things, which Zimbardo stated as "The Lucifer Effect," there is something more important here. Zimbardo also concluded that people can do violent things due to situational influences and power given from authority. He also stated that, *They can also be led to act in irrational, stupid, self-destructive, antisocial, and mindless ways when they are immersed in "total situations" that impact human nature in ways that challenge our sense of stability and consistency of individual personality, of character, and of morality.*

Essentially, we're all capable of violent acts, but it's not violence that is bad, it's our intentions, situations and what society deems "bad" that makes our violent nature either "good" or "bad." This also means we can control our violent behavior.

The power is in the system. The system creates the situation that corrupts the individual. The system is the legal, political, economic, cultural background. ... If you want to change the person, you have to change the situation, if you want to change the situation, you have to know where the power is in the system. - Philip Zimbardo

The best way to understand ourselves and our natural tendencies and emotions is to study our history and human nature throughout evolution and why we've become who we are. Take away violence from the human species at any point in history and we don't exist, we become extinct immediately. Thankfully the need for violence in our country has been nearly eliminated as we have fairly easy access to life's necessities and safeguards from predators. Understand that it is due to our violent nature that we have a more peaceful world now than ever before in our history. Our military is a big part of this reason. They are trained to tap into that violence and use it in a way that the rest of us don't want to or are afraid of.

While we may not have a need for violence these days, that doesn't mean that the violent part of us suddenly disappears or even diminishes, it's still there, and it must still come out. We can't let violence come out whenever just to alleviate or satisfy that violent part of us. We need to teach ourselves, our children, and our society, how to control this urge when it's not needed. We fail miserably at this.

When I was much younger, grade school age to junior high school, I had a tough time with anger. Occasionally, I got into a fight, be it verbally or physically, but mostly I just held it in as I was told numerous times over not to fight. I badly wanted to punch a lot of people though. Instead, I grumbled my way through it, letting it fester for days on end.

Not only did it effect my life during the time I was letting it fester, it was the only thing on my mind. Forget about studying or enjoying time with friends. I let my anger explode by yelling at friends or arguing with my father, or throwing my baseball helmet into the dugout swearing how that wasn't a strike, then arguing with a teammate or coach.

Luckily I held my composure most days and didn't let it get out of hand, but that just meant it ate me up even more on the inside. I needed to get that rage and anger out, but had no way to do it aside from smashing a baseball with the bat, but refer to the strike out above on how that attempt usually ended. Then I found my venting place, my cure-all, in 1994 as I walked into my new home away from home, the dojang.

How do we control our violence? In my opinion, the same way we control our emotions. We're told not to hold in our emotions, but to let them out in a proper manner. Yet we are told to never let out our violent nature. How is this any different? Holding it in only leads to frustration and it always finds its way out, but without your control or desire to let it out.

The violent nature we hold in is pent up and eventually finds a way out, and usually it's not in the good way. While I'm sure there are numerous ways of getting this violence out, such as art, writing, and physical exercise, I'm a firm believer that martial arts training is the best format if done correctly. Emphasis on the words, "done correctly."

If not done correctly, we are just providing tools of destruction to an already untamed beast. While I'm an advocate of protecting our children from viewing or experiencing violent acts, in particular the bad kind, this alone is not enough to control our violent nature. Simply protecting or ignoring it will not keep it from happening. I speak with my youth students everyday about their actions and go to great lengths to control these spurts of uncontrolled violent actions. It comes out in many ways, such as yelling in anger, shutting down and separating themselves from others, or physical actions such as pushing or striking another out of anger or retaliation. Even the best students have moments of acting out in a bad way as they simply don't know how to control it otherwise. Physical training must be accompanied by the mental training of understanding oneself and others in order to control our violent nature.

Yes, times change and society and our rules and our thoughts on what's morally correct may change, but our physical being hasn't changed at the same pace. Even if we find peace throughout the entire world in the next hundred years, our violent nature will still remain. It could take hundreds of thousands of years to evolve out of something like that. Until that time comes, embrace your violent nature as a gift that has helped you survive, and train it properly so it never goes beyond your control and destroys you or those around you. Only through violence have we found peace in our history. It may not be what we want or what we are proud of, but it is what it is, and we must understand it better than we do now to progress towards further peace.

CHAPTER 45

There is no hero known as the man of tin

Class photo with Dan's after school students in 2019. Photo by Jen Van Kirk.

Discipline vs. A Discipline. While these aren't necessarily different, the way we think of them is. Martial arts and discipline go hand in hand. But that doesn't mean if you send your out of control children to a martial arts school that they will suddenly be whipped into shape and turned into obedient little angels. Martial arts is A discipline. It takes focus, concentration, determination, perseverance, and a respect for it in order to advance through it and be successful. We can certainly instill discipline into a child but it will take time and teamwork.

Years ago, I had a parent bring their seven-year-old into the dojang for a trial class. The mother was very sweet and the child seemed to be nice as well. However, the child wasn't thrilled about taking martial arts classes and didn't want to do it once there. The mother really wanted him to attend as he had some discipline and control issues. She promised the child that he could go to a local arcade and play zone if he took the class and behaved. He begrudgingly accepted.

Class started fairly well and he had some good talent. About halfway through class we started working on some stances/footwork and he didn't want to do it anymore. He then ran over to the wall, plugged his ears and screamed. I refused to give in and let him go and began focusing my efforts on another child who wanted to learn.

I've had similar things happen before. What I've learned is that the kids do this to get their way. If you ignore them, they eventually get tired and give in. If you give them the open door to come back and participate in class, most will take that open door as it becomes their decision rather than it being forced upon them by the instructor or parent.

Sadly, just seconds into this hissy fit, the mother ran onto my floor and over to him to plead for him to stop. He ignored her and continued to scream. She then instantly gave in to him and said, "Okay, okay, we'll leave and go to the arcade if you just stop screaming." To no one's surprise, he immediately halted, the screaming ended, and was all smiles and a perfect little saint again. I just stood and stared in bafflement. "There's your problem," I uttered to myself as they left.

I've had numerous parents over the years bring their children to me because he/she is out of control, lacks discipline, doesn't do what they are told, is disrespectful, etc. They all want me to miraculously correct these issues. While I'm glad the parent chose to bring their child to a martial arts school to help change behaviors, I find that many parents simply want to drop the kids off expecting a quick fix. This simply isn't going to happen. As a result, most quick fix parents remove their children from classes after a month of occasionally getting them to classes and seeing no improvement.

Keep in mind that as an instructor, I only work with a child for one to three hours a day for maybe a few days. In many cases, it's once or twice a week for an hour. I don't train students under the age of six-years-old, therefore, when they do come to me, they have at least six years of learned behavior. There is nothing legal I can do to correct this child's behavior in such a short amount of time. And even if there was, it wouldn't last. Give me a few years, then yes, you'll see remarkable improvement. But a month or two of casually taking classes is not enough. Correcting a behavior takes considerable time. Whether it's a physical movement or a mental behavior, it just doesn't happen instantly.

At home, as it is in the Dojang. One thing that causes massive setbacks when correcting a child's behavior through martial arts is that much of what I teach in class is negated at home. I have strict rules at my studio; from acknowledging a command by saying "Yes Sir!" to showing respect for everyone in the studio, as well as, the studio itself (taking time to clean it,) showing manners and common courtesy. The students get punished when they step out of line and rewarded when doing things right.

Sadly, these same rules are not being regularly applied at home, and in some cases, are completely negated by parents rewarding bad behavior. All this does, at best, is set boundaries where the child is supposed to behave, in the studio, and where they don't have to behave, at home and everywhere else. If you're a parent of a problem child and you have them enrolled in martial arts to help correct the bad behavior, that's excellent. Just make sure you know the rules that are set in the studio and be consistent with them being active all day outside of the studio.

I find that training a child and training a dog are nearly identical, but with a few exceptions: 1. Most children don't like the taste of dog biscuits; 2. Society frowns upon using a choke chain on your dog; 3. While rubbing a child's nose in a mess they made works well, it tends to upset the parents; 4. Dogs have unconditional love. Okay, I'm joking, sort of, but you get the point.

I see people put more effort into training their pets than they do their own children and it's quite strange to me. We have this notion that children will grow up correctly on their own, and that the child's school, daycare, martial arts school, nanny or someone else will teach them right and wrong, but it doesn't work that way. We all teach differently and teach different aspects and skill sets. The foundation of proper behavior must be set at home and extended elsewhere.

One thing that I've noticed is that the children that come to me well behaved and find great success in martial arts all tend to have parents that are actively involved in their lives in a positive way. It's not easy obviously, as people have to pay the bills and support their families and that can lead to very little time with their children. I don't have the answer to this, as I am not a parent. All I can do is point out what I see as the outsider who trains your children.

The man of steel. There is an old adage in martial arts that a friend and fellow instructor reminded me of one day. "We turn tin into steel," he proclaimed. I remember hearing this, and similar sayings many years ago but it was lost on me at the time as I spent most of my time working with and training adults. But now that I'm working with more youth students, some are here because they are coerced by their parents, while others aspire to be the next power ranger, that adage is in full force.

As an instructor, we sometimes feel like we are putting more effort into helping these kids, than they are willing to do themselves. We beat our heads against the wall trying to figure out what we, as instructors, are doing wrong. We come up with new punishments, new rewards, new drills, and new ways of saying the same thing for the millionth time that clearly hasn't been heard. And nothing works. We do our best to turn these flimsy pieces of tin into steel. But we have to remember the second half of the adage, "But first, the tin must want to become steel." And therein lies the issue.

There isn't much we can do until the student shows a willingness to learn and improve. As an instructor, our first objective is to give the child a reason to want to learn, or alter their behavior. This, of course, is easier said than done. But it can be done, and it must be done before progress is made.

For many students, the instructor must constantly remind them of these internal desires. I've never had many high ranking youth students. Most of these students become teenagers by the time they reach those upper ranks, even if they had started at a young age. These are the students who want to change and have put the effort into changing. I do not hand out belts just because the student has paid, nor do I reward lackluster effort. My belt ranks are earned.

To gain rank as a martial artist, especially to gain a black belt or junior black belt, you must actively change who you are, not just physically, but mentally and spiritually. My failure as an instructor comes when I am unable to convince a student to want to turn from tin to steel. However, when I do convince them, and their parents and I are on the same track, I know a life is about to be forever changed for the better.

EPILOGUE

The used couch, sacrifices, and the procrastinating contrarian

Dan's used and tattered couch that he built his office around. Photo by Dan Bourelle.

In 2008, I decided to go from part time to full time with my martial arts studio. I had lost my job with the Architectural and Engineering Firm and had to decide between moving to find another job in the same field in the middle of the recession or staying in Wilmington, a city I love and continue training the small handful of loyal evening students. It was not an easy decision for me, particularly during the height of the recession. It's not only incredibly difficult to start any business, but to start a business that is all about what most mistakenly consider an expendable activity is close to insane.

I looked at my life and what I had on the line to lose if things didn't go well. I didn't have any children or anyone to take care of or be responsible for, but I had my house, my car, and random things I don't have much attachment to. I decided that my house, car, and the rest, weren't as important as my dream of teaching martial arts for a living. I wanted job security that I had control over to support my ultimate goal, having a family.

I assumed that I would most likely lose my house. Banks were not giving out loans at the time so I had to do it all myself from the little I had saved. My first purchase was a used couch. In the event I lost my house, I would have a place to sleep as I planned on living in my studio if necessary. I had found the perfect couch on craigslist that fit into my office. I called up the owner and told him I wanted to buy it. He said he had just loaded it up into a U-Haul® and asked me to buy it from him at the flea market the next morning. I begged him to let me come right over to get it and I would unpack it personally if needed as I couldn't make it the next day and it was the only couch that fit my office. He begrudgingly accepted and began explaining where he was located. It sounded familiar, very familiar. I asked his address, which he gave me.

Then I took a step out onto my front porch and looked to my left and waved at my neighbor who had just loaded up his couch into his U-Haul and was on the phone, with me! Of the hundreds of couches on craigslist in a city of well over seventy thousand, it was my neighbor's that had the perfect couch!

We laughed and he actually drove it over to my studio for me and helped carry it into the office. Crazy good luck! It was a sign, even though I don't believe in signs or fate or any of that, but moments like that make me wonder. Years later, as I leased a new building for my studio, I actually designed the layout of my new office to fit that couch. It's old, it's ugly, I rarely use it, and I have no interest in ever getting rid of it. It was a symbol of the chance I took and what could have been if I didn't work so hard to make it work. These sacrifices I was willing to make to live my dream seemed one hundred percent worth it!

I worked relentlessly the first couple of years with my full time studio. In addition, I did personal training for supplemental income, and rented out my studio to fitness groups during hours I wasn't there teaching. My first training clients were at five in the morning and continued through the morning and into the afternoon most days before doing my own workout. When I didn't have clients, I had morning and noon hour classes, and boot camps I was teaching at the studio.

After a quick midafternoon lunch, I had my first martial arts classes to teach for the day around three thirty and had back to back adult classes until nine o'clock at night, at which time I cleaned up and closed up and headed home to eat dinner. It was around ten o'clock before sitting at the computer and responding to emails or to work up advertisements. I usually made it to bed around midnight, sometimes later, only to wake up at four in the morning to do it all again the next day.

Hard work is a prison sentence only if it does not have meaning. Once it does, it becomes the kind of thing that makes you grab your wife around the waist and dance a jig. – Malcolm Gladwell

I had begun sacrificing a lot in an effort to build my school. Sleep was slim to none. So much so that I had serious insomnia to the point of hallucinating that shadow people were in my room at night. I sacrificed buying anything that wasn't needed. I had my personal expenses (which includes food) down under two hundred dollars a month. No clothes, no electronics or other non-essential items, nothing. No vacations. I watched what few relationships and friendships I had slip away into, "people I know and get along with on the rare occasion I see them." While I would have truly loved to have those friendships, relationships, and things - so to speak, I willingly let them go because I believed it would allow me to build the best school possible and that it would only be temporary. The key word being, believed.

Year after year, I pushed back the vacations, the friends, and the items that enrich our lives, as I made only minor improvements each year. It was not big enough to be self-sustaining. I did, however, begin to try and take portions of my life back by working a little smarter and cutting down on the number of classes and clients I had in order to live a little and get back some of my sleep and sanity. Sadly, eleven years later, the effects of my decisions to sacrifice so much for my business has led to a shortage of some of the most crucial things that make up the best parts of life. My desire to have a family and a solid social network has been nearly destroyed due to my sacrifices. These sacrifices were not worth it.

My writing has been a welcome outlet for me when not training or teaching. However, it has also been a small part of what has taken me away from the lifestyle I had dreamed of. I decided to sacrifice one more summer to compile my stories and blogs, and finalize this book so I can finally scratch this off my to-do list.

I've dragged it on far too long due to my perfectionist mindset and worries that it won't be good enough or that someone may hate it, overlooking those that might actually enjoy it. I've written a lot about my mistakes. I've shown you how I've adjusted and described those eureka moments. I hope I've motivated students and others in these pages. I tried to give you things to think about and mull over. I've called out procrastinations and faults in what I've seen from students or just people in general.

I've taken some contrarian points of view in some cases as I truly enjoy trying to find the unconventional answers to difficult questions. I see other people that spend the day talking about how to live one's life or posting motivational quotes on social media attempting to make prolific and unique statements. For some, I think to myself, "Why don't they take their own advice?"

In my head I've named these people "Procrastinating Contrarians." Yet, the harshest failure and the toughest criticism I have is of myself, and that isn't easy to admit. I've made an effort to maintain that my sacrifices were helping my business. The biggest failure is not recognizing that I am the Procrastinating Contrarian. It took the process of rereading and compiling all of my writings to realize this.

I write this for the same reason I've written all of these chapters, to teach others so they can learn from my mistakes and failures. I also write this final chapter to close a chapter in my life and at least try and find a new path. Our culture assumes that hard work and sacrifice are the only way to succeed. While that can be the case, it has to be worthwhile hard work and proper sacrifices. Looking back, not all of my hard work was helping grow my business. It may have been under the umbrella of "for my school," but that doesn't mean it was helping grow the school. Working smart, not hard, as they say.

Only in recent years have I realized that the most successful martial arts instructors are also the most socially successful. They have significant others, children, and a large circle of friends. I wanted these things too, but made the mistake in thinking that by making the school successful it would make it easier to find these things. It seems I was wrong!

As it relates to my students, or anyone reading this, make sure and keep your eye on the real goals. While having a big successful school is a high priority for me, having a family and good close friends was always a bigger goal. I see this with students in classes as well. It's easy to get caught up on a technique that they are struggling with and placing all of their effort into that technique. I've watched them get flustered, frustrated and in some cases give up and walk away. In many cases though, that technique isn't even that important as it relates to the larger goal. Sometimes students can get so in the woods with the small detail in the technique that they forget to just make it ugly sometimes to get it to work rather than trying to make it perfect.

It's important to take a step back every so often or even let something go for a while and come back to it later with a fresh view and renewed effort. Sacrifices are generally needed in all aspects of life. However, just because we sacrifice something, doesn't mean we'll automatically achieve our goal. It must be a calculated sacrifice when needed, and never sacrifice your ultimate goal. It sounds so stupid to do when it's written down or spoken, but sometimes so hard to do when you've got your nose to the grindstone and never pause to think. Take it from me, the biggest procrastinating contrarian of them all.

CONCLUSION

Part of why it took me so long to write this book was trying to find a way to compile and connect all of these blogs turned chapters. Upon rereading many of my past blogs, many of which I had completely forgotten about, and was convinced someone else wrote them and slipped them in, I had noticed a common theme. Failure turned to success or realization. In most scenarios, it was my failure.

Writing this book was a humbling process that I had to fight at times. It's not easy telling everyone how you blew it, especially students. What I've noticed over the years, as I've been releasing my writing in newsletter form for eight years, is that my students have responded in a positive way because of them. While I have received some backlash from some of my opinions over the more controversial subjects, I've always had calm and open discussions with these people and felt that both parties came away more enlightened. I know I sure have. I've altered some of my views since first posting them as mistakes were pointed out. We, as instructors, do our best never to make mistakes and to try and always have the answers for our students so as to give the perception that we are perfect in every way.

Not only is that an impossible task, it's self-destructive and even holds students back by presenting them with the impossible task of attempting to be the fake perfect person that you present. No student can obtain this, and it can hold them back and negatively affect their training or mental state by believing there's no hope. By writing up excerpts to send out as a newsletter to students, it has promoted useful questions in class as well as shown my students that I have failed, and continue to fail constantly in order to succeed. It promotes honesty in my classroom, and that honesty can help break down barriers that can hold not just students back, but myself as a practitioner and instructor.

One big point I want to get across through this book is not to state that all failure leads to success, but to learn to accept that failure is part of the equation and to see the silver linings when things don't go according to plan. Use that failure as a way to improve yourself or the situation somehow.

As I make the final adjustments to this book to send to the publisher for editing, we are currently in the middle of a pandemic due to Covid-19, aka, the corona virus. My studio has been forced to shut down. My income has been shut down. Yet, all of my bills continue to add up. The first couple of weeks I was in a downward spiral knowing that I had no way to pay the bills to keep my school alive and may end up closing my studio, my livelihood, and everything I've spent the last sixteen years building from the ground up.

However, even in my darkest moments, I've done two things consistently. Keep improving my system and studio by finishing projects I've had on the back burner until I had more time. The second, is to find ways to keep laughing. While some days laughing is a difficult task, I find ways to do it.

Due to these improvements I've made, when I reopen my school, it will be dramatically improved and with a new sense of enthusiasm and mindset on how to better prepare for the future and any other similar issues that may arise.

Has this pandemic failure led to me succeeding? Probably not anytime soon. It will most likely take a year or two to bounce back to some form of normal. However, I will be better prepared and my students will receive an even higher quality service from me due to this. So, while this shutdown has been atrocious and has me on the brink of losing everything, I know I'll be better for it when I come out on the other side. That is the essence of this book. Don't let failure be permanent, but let it be an opportunity for self-improvement.

One of the biggest surprise elements, however, has come from the editing and compiling process to turn these blogs into a book. By the time I finished compiling the book, I had come to realize that I wasn't just talking to my students, but I was talking to myself. On a subconscious level, I was telling myself what I need to do or calling out my former heavily flawed self to not make the same mistakes in the future. With this knowledge, I'd like to leave you with a promise and a suggestion.

Knowing that I will continue to stumble into failure, be it from my own mistakes or through happenstance, I promise to neither hide nor ignore them in an effort to turn them into a learning experience. I may even gleefully continue to write about my failures for all to laugh and learn from when the opportunity arises. My suggestion to you is to learn from my failures, as well as others around you, in order to navigate to the path of success. When you see a friend get burned by sticking their hand into the fire, you don't need to stick your own hand in that flame to learn that all bare hands get burned from the fire!

Now go forth and fail your way to success, my fellow Dan-Do practitioners!

Glossary

Aikido – A traditional Japanese martial art known for its use of non-resistance to create throws, deflections, trips, and joint locks. *Ai* means to "harmonize" or "coordinate," *ki* loosely means "life force" or "energy," and *do* means "the way." Therefore, *Aikido* means "The Way of harmonizing Life Energy."

American Taekwondo Association (ATA) – One of the largest Taekwondo organizations in the world. Founded in 1969 by Haeng Ung Lee.

Autonomic Nervous System (ANS) – A bodily system that primarily controls involuntary functions such as the heart rate and digestion.

Board Breaking – A technique used in some martial arts systems that involves breaking board using various kicks or strikes to demonstrate skill and power.

Board Spacers – A spacer used to separate two boards, or other breaking material, to create space between boards. Typically about one quarter inch in thickness.

Circular motion – A philosophy used by the martial art of Hapkido that involves moving oneself or limb in a circular motion.

Closed-Loop Motor Control – A feedback system, based on trial and error, used by the body to learn the most efficient way to perform a muscular movement, such as throwing a punch.

Dobok – The Korean term used to refer to the uniform worn in martial arts.

Dojang - Korean term for the physical place of training for martial arts practitioners.

Federation – A term used to define a governing body that resides over a group of schools, usually of the same martial arts style.

Feint – A fake attack used to see your opponents reaction to said technique.

Flow like water – A philosophy used by the martial art of Hapkido that involves moving from one defense to another seamlessly rather than forcing a technique to work through resistance.

Flurry – Quick and numerous attacks in succession.

Forms – A term used to describe a sequence of movements involving martial arts techniques. Also known as a poomse, pattern, or kata.

Ge-Baek – A pattern performed in the black belt ranks in ITF Taekwon-Do named after General Ge-Baek in the Korean Army during the Baekje Dynasty. Before entering an unwinnable battle, he supposedly killed his wife and children so they would not fall into enemy hands and be tortured, and to make sure his only focus was on the battle and not his family. The pattern represents his severe and strict military discipline that he demonstrated.

Grappling – The act of grabbing an opponent in an effort to control them in some manner. Generally associated with martial arts styles that make use of throws, joint locks, and ground defense.

Gumdo – A traditional Korean martial art specializing in the Jingum, a Korean sword similar to a Samurai sword. *Gum* means, "sword" and *do* means "the way." Therefore, *Gumdo* means "The Way of the Sword." Also known as Kumdo.

Hamstring – The term used to describe the three major muscles (Bicep Femoris, Semimembranosus, and Semitendinosus) that make up the back of the upper leg.

Hapkido – A traditional Korean martial art that specializes in joint locks as well as making use of kicking, striking, throwing, ground defense, weapons, and pressure points. *Hap* means, "Coordinated" or "Harmonizing," *ki* loosely means "Power," and *do* means "The way." Generally interpreted as "the way of coordinated power."

Insert – The folded booklet inside cassette tapes, CD's, and other forms of media, which lists information about the media such as musicians, producers, and lyrics.

International Taekwondo Federation (ITF) – One of the largest Taekwondo organizations in the world. Founded in 1955 by General Choi Hong Hi.

Jingum – A long, slightly curved Korean sword used in the martial arts of Gumdo.

Joint Lock – A technique used in many grappling style martial arts that involves locking a joint in a manner in which it's not meant to bend in order to create pain or leverage to gain control of an attacker.

Karate – A traditional Japanese martial art that focuses on unarmed combat, primarily through strikes and kicks. *Kara* means "empty" and *Te* means "Hands." Thus, it is the art of "Empty Hands."

Kata – The Japanese term of a sequence of movements involving martial arts techniques. Also known as a form, pattern, or Poomse.

Ki/Chi – While there is no direct translation or word for it in English, it is loosely translated to an invisible power, life force, or strength within the body. *Ki* relates to the Korean culture and *Chi* relates to the Chinese culture, both having similar meanings.

Makiwara board – A board with a tough surface, such as rope or canvas, that martial artists strike to toughen up the striking point by creating calluses, strengthen the joints involved, and potentially create small breaks in the bone that repair stronger.

Masters Ceremony – A ceremony performed in some associations when a practitioner has earned the title of Master.

Master Instructor – A term reserved for seasoned martial arts instructors who have mastered the art they teach. Generally only given to those that are very high rank in their art and have dedicated approximately twenty years of training and training in their chosen art.

Moo Hahn Hahn Hapkido – A modern style of Hapkido that holds no restrictions on techniques. Moo Hahn Hahn means "boundless" or "unrestrained." It is "The Unrestrained Art of Hapkido."

MMA – An acronym for Mixed Martial Arts. A generally used term for training in multiple martial arts styles. Also referred to when describing sport fighting.

Non-resistance – A philosophy used by the martial art of Hapkido that involves moving with forces rather than against forces.

One Step – A predetermined defense against an attack that is trained in many Taekwondo and Gum-Do martial arts styles. The one step refers to an attack that involves only one attack or "step" such as a punch or a kick. Also known as One Step Sparring.

Open-Loop Motor Control – A system that is the result of the closed-loop motor control feedback system. It provides a quick response to perform a muscular movement, such as throwing a punch, but without the feedback response used in the closed-loop system.

Parasympathetic Nervous System (PNS) – A bodily system under the umbrella of the autonomic nervous system that controls regulatory involuntary functions such as digestion while the body is at rest, compared to under stress.

Patterns – A term used to describe a sequence of movements involving martial arts techniques. Also known as a form, poomse, or kata.

Point Sparring – A competitive style of sparring, used mostly by Karate and Taekwondo, that involves kicking or striking the opponent to gain enough points to win the match.

Poomse – The Korean term of a sequence of movements involving martial arts techniques. Also known as a form, pattern, or kata.

PTSD – An acronym for Post-Traumatic Stress Disorder. A disorder that is created from experiencing or witnessing a traumatic event in which a person has flashbacks or other negative effects from the event well after the situation.

Sabumnim – Korean term for instructor. Similar to Sensei in Japanese arts.

Self-Defense Scenarios - A training element that involves any staged scenario where self-defense would be used in a rehearsed or impromptu way. Examples: Being attacked by multiple attackers, attackers with weapons, or protecting another student from an attacker.

Sine Wave – The name of the power generation used

primarily in Taekwondo. It involves an up and down movement with the body and involves timing of a strike with the use of body weight and gravity. Also known as sine wave motion or just wave motion.

Songham Forms – "Pine tree and Rock," and is also the name of the form set used by the American Taekwondo Association.

S.W.A.T. – An acronym for Special Weapons and Tactics. A special group within law enforcement that is called into action during extremely volatile and potentially violent situations.

Sympathetic Nervous System (SNS) – A bodily system under the umbrella of the autonomic nervous system that controls the involuntary actions triggered by the body's reaction to some sort of stress. This system is in control of homeostasis in the body, such as regulating body temperature. This also controls the "fight, flight, or freeze" reaction which can create adrenaline dumps, vasoconstriction, and tunnel vision for survival in perceived life or death situations.

Tai Chi – A traditional Chinese martial arts known for its slow, meditative movements. Also known as Taichi Quan or Taiji Quan, or "Grand Ultimate Fist."

Taekwondo – A traditional Korean martial art that focuses primarily on kicking and striking. *Tae* means 'foot,' *kwon* means "fist' and *do* means "the way." Hence known as "The way of foot and fist fighting."

Taeguk – The red and blue symbol used on the Korean National Flag to represent balance. The red half represents positive forces and the blue represents the negative.

Taeguk Forms – The Korean symbol of balance, it is also the name of the form set used by the World Taekwondo or WT.

Testing - Also known as a rank exam. Testings are generally a formal class in which an instructor, or panel of judges test students over their material and skills to determine if they are ready to be promoted to a higher rank.

U.F.C. – Ultimate Fighting Championship, a sport fighting promotion based in Las Vegas, NV.

VHS – Video Home System. A cassette-like item used to view movies and other recorded videos. Similar to a DVD disc.

World Taekwondo (WT) – One of the largest Taekwondo organizations in the world as well as the governing association of sport Taekwondo that is used in the Olympics, among other places. Founded in 1973.

Yin/Yang – A Chinese philosophical symbol representing balance or dualism. Yin is the black portion of the symbol and represents the negative, feminine, and passive attributes. The Yang is the white portion of the symbol representing the positive, masculine, and active attributes. Both work together to create balance and are equal and needed parts of a whole.

REFERENCES

The Book of Five Rings, by Miyamoto Musashi

The Art of Harmony, by Sang H. Kim

Nei Jia Quan, by Jess O'Brien

The Art of Expressing the Human Body, by John Little

Meditations on Violence, by Rory Miller

The Gift of Fear, by Gavin De Becker

Cornell Study: The Accuracy of Inferences about Criminality Based on Facial Appearance, by Jeffrey Valla, Stephen Ceci, and Wendy Williams, published in the Journal of Social, Evolutionary and Cultural Psychology (Vol. 5:1)

Outliers: The Story of Success, by Malcolm Gladwell

The Stanford Prison Experiment, conducted by Philip Zimbardo

Get Some Headspace, How Mindfulness Can Change Your Life in Ten Minutes a Day, by Andy Puddicombe

On Combat, by Dave Grossman

How NOT to get HIT: The Art of Fighting Without Fighting, by Nathaniel Cooke

ABOUT THE AUTHOR

After a number of years competing in martial arts throughout the mid-western and southeastern United States, Master Daniel Lee Bourelle has settled into teaching full time in Wilmington, N.C. where he owns and operates his martial arts studio, Bourelle Martial Arts. As of 2020 he holds the ranks of sixth degree black belt in Hapkido, fifth degree black belt in Taekwondo, and a third degree black belt in Gumdo. He is also the founder of Moo Hahn Hahn Hapkido, which was created upon heavily altering his Hapkido program in 2013. Master Bourelle also works with clients as a fitness trainer, specializing in correctional exercises.

For more information on Bourelle Martial Arts and its services

Contact Information

Studio Phone: (910) 264-3486

Email: dan@bourellemartialarts.com

Website: www.bourellemartialarts.com

After-School Website: https://afterschoolbma.com/

Sign up for our Monthly Newsletter for scheduled events, enrollment specials, and new blog posts.

Services

Martial Arts Programs:

Moo Hahn Hahn Hapkido

Taekwondo

Gumdo

After-School Martial Arts Program

Self-Defense Seminars and Courses

Personal Training

Private Lessons

Online martial arts classes

Martially Motivated Podcast

Master Bourelle discusses all things martial arts, such as prevention and awareness as well as great stories with fellow martial artists that join in on the podcast. This podcast can be found on the Bourelle Martial Arts website among other podcast apps.

Follow Bourelle Martial Arts on Facebook, Instagram and Twitter.